whizz it

MURDOCH BOOKS

contents

whizzing it

Food processing appliances are designed to simplify cooking, but while you'll find one lurking in most home kitchens, few cooks use them to full advantage. Such a shame when a little frenzied whizzing can be so therapeutic. Not to mention the fact that with minimal time and fuss, and some gentle coaxing, they can assist in creating some rather spectacular dishes. Discover how versatile your food processor, blender, immersion blender, coffee grinder or spice mill can be as you blend, chop, purée, mix, grind, crush and whip at the touch of a button. Follow the simple methods to whizz up a gorgeous blend of flavours and variety of textures, and enjoy some classic favourites and delicious new treats. Hold on tight ... you'll be whizzing up a storm in no time.

the machines

Although there are now myriad specialist machines available, such as milkshake makers, liquidizers and juicers, we're concentrating on those general purpose whizzers that have the versatility to allow a number of applications and more importantly, those that are found in most kitchens.

We recommend those machines that are best suited to each recipe, but you can substitute one machine for another; for example, use a blender instead of an immersion blender for soups, or a food processor instead of a blender for shakes.

the immersion blender

Also known as hand-held or wand blenders, these are ideal for whizzing soft solids or liquids in a vessel, often the pan in which the ingredients have been cooking. Most have two speeds, and some also come with a blade for whipping and one for blending, as well as the general purpose chopping blade. Results are dependent on the machine being slowly moved through the ingredients, which gives a certain degree of control. Convenience is a big feature, as the ingredients don't have to be moved from one vessel to another to be blended, and there is often just the shaft and blade to wash.

the blender

Designed for liquids and soft solids, the ubiquitous blender is the most straightforward of the group. With a fixed blade set in a narrow base and a tall, narrow bowl, the ingredients are efficiently lifted and circulated for uniform blending. The narrow base also means that blenders can handle small volumes — the perfect example of a case where size doesn't matter. The average capacity is 1.5 litres (52 fl oz/6 cups).

the coffee grinder or spice mill

These are compact machines with a small built-in bowl and a powerful motor that operates at one speed. They have a fixed (non-removable) blade that is blunted and set at an angle to grind rather than chop. Not designed for liquids, the bowl will take 3–4 tablespoons of dry solids such as coffee beans or whole spices.

the mini processor

With a small detachable bowl, mini processors can take up to 250 ml (9 fl oz/ 1 cup) of liquid. They usually have one multipurpose metal blade attachment, but sometimes this has a double side, for either chopping or grinding, depending on the direction in which you run the machine. They operate at just one speed: very fast. Most mini processors have two small holes in the cover to release air. This also allows for liquids to be added (through one hole only) at a controlled rate while the motor is running, which is invaluable for making emulsions such as mayonnaise or hollandaise sauce.

the processor

These come in varying sizes, but will fall into one of two categories: small, which will safely process 1 litre (35 fl oz/4 cups) of liquid, and a larger version that can handle 1.5–1.75 litres (52–61 fl oz/6–7 cups) of liquid. Manufacturers differ in their description of the machine's capacity — some give the actual capacity of the bowl, while others go by the recommended optimum operating capacity, and/or the solids capacity. Large processors often come with a metal blade for chopping and a plastic blade for mixing, and they may have whisking, shredding or grating attachments. Small processors are more likely to have just one general purpose blade. They both operate at variable speeds, and there are now machines available that can run at relatively slow, low speeds. Processors have a minimum working volume. If there is too little in the machine, it will be whizzed out to the side of the bowl, beyond the reach of the blade.

processors

Many processors come with a number of accessories,

such as different blades and grating and slicing discs.

Mini processors are ideal for chopping nuts or herbs,

or blending small quantities of liquids.

blenders
and grinders

Immersion blenders and whisks allow you to whizz food in

the cooking pan. Spice mills are good for grinding whole

spices, and blenders make quick work of drinks and shakes.

whizzing basics

blend it

To blend liquids and soft ingredients efficiently, a fast speed, a metal blade and a well-designed bowl are required. These features aerate the mixture and help to give a light texture. One look at the common blender, a design that has remained virtually unchanged since its conception, tells the story, but blending is also successful in a food processor fitted with the metal blade, or with an immersion blender fitted with the blending attachment. When blending semi-solids, blend in short bursts initially to break them down, then run the motor continuously until the desired texture is reached.

chop it

The best results when chopping ingredients are achieved by chopping in short bursts with the metal chopping or general purpose blade. This action allows the ingredients to briefly settle on the base of the bowl after each pulse, thus bringing them in contact with the blade each time. It also enables you to check the progress of the chopping as you go. Processing small amounts in batches will ensure even chopping.

purée it

This is the ultimate whizzing action for soups, sauces, mashes and fruits. If a machine whizzes, it purées — just switch it to high speed and go for it. However, it's recommended that you whizz in short bursts two-thirds of the way through so that you have some control over the finished texture.

mix it

A processor fitted with the plastic blade is ideal for mixing because it doesn't cut the ingredients, such as the fruit in a fruit cake batter. Use the slowest speed and keep the motor running continuously. Mixing can also be done in a blender or in a processor fitted with the metal general purpose blade, as long as there is nothing in the mixture that needs to remain uncut. It is recommended that liquids be added with the motor running.

grind it

This is the ideal application for coffee beans, nuts, grains and whole spices. A blunted metal blade, used in good electric coffee and spice mills, grinds rather than chops to give a fine powdery texture. Some mini processors have a grinding function that runs the motor in reverse and uses a blunted edge on the back of the sharp cutting blade. Grinding works best with the motor running continuously.

crush it

Ice cubes can be crushed by using the metal blade and chopping in short bursts initially, then finished off at high continuous speed. When making drinks, the ice cubes can be crushed at the same time as the liquids are mixed, but with chilled soups and iced desserts the crushing is best done separately. Work in batches if necessary, and keep an eye on the progress because overprocessing can melt the ice. Starting with small, uniform ice cubes gives even crushing.

whip it

Some processors have an aerator or whisking attachment designed for whipping cream and whisking egg whites. Whizz continuously on the slowest speed possible, and stop as soon as the desired volume is reached; it's easy to overprocess at these high speeds. Note that volumes may not be as great as when using conventional whipping methods.

cream it

Creaming butter and sugar or mixing egg yolks with sugar is best done at low speed using a plastic blade in a small bowl; if the bowl is too big the mixture will just get whizzed to the base and side of the bowl, beyond the reach of the blade.

caring for your machine

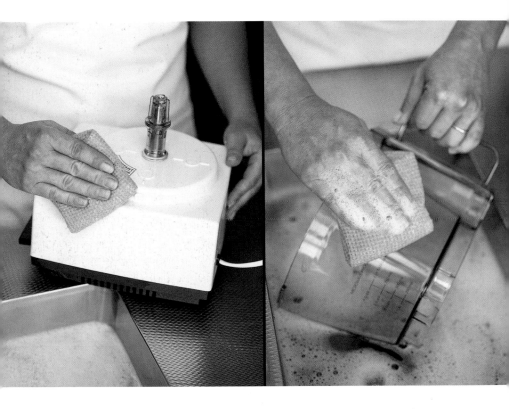

Wash immediately after use to prevent food staining or crusting, and be careful **not to immerse** any part of the motor body in water.

Avoid using scourers or **abrasive cleaners** on any part of the machine, particularly the plastic bowls, as they may damage the surface.

Always **wipe dry** completely before packing away, especially parts that are stored fitted together. This applies particularly to the inside of the attachment shaft.

Do not store the machine with the lid locked in the ON position. This puts **unnecessary strain** on the operating switch.

15

hints and tips

■ Although whizzing times are suggested in each recipe, bear in mind that they are only approximate and will depend on factors such as the speed of the machine, the sharpness of the blade and the moisture content of the ingredients.

■ Processors and blenders work best when the bowl is half full of liquid, or two-thirds full of solids such as cake mix or vegetables. Overloading will lead to spillages and inconsistent processing.

■ Immersion blenders should be used in deep, narrow vessels that are half full to avoid splattering.

■ For best results when blending with an immersion blender, hold it at an angle and draw it up slowly through the liquid.

■ To prevent splattering, always turn off immersion blenders before lifting them from the ingredients.

■ Use the plastic blade on the processor when you wish to retain texture; for example, when mixing ricotta cheese or chunky tomato sauces.

■ It's good practice to always attend your machine during operation. Don't walk away while the motor is running — machines have been known to travel across the bench and topple off.

■ When adding ingredients with the motor running, do not stop the motor until everything has been added and the desired consistency is reached.

■ Avoid overprocessing, which can alter the texture and sometimes the nature of the ingredient; for example, cream could become butter or ground nuts could turn into a paste.

■ It is often necessary to stop mid-whizzing and scrape mixture down off the side of the bowl. This is best done using a plastic or rubber spatula.

■ As a safety measure, never operate a processor or blender continuously for more than 1 minute.

- When making emulsions using a mini processor with holes in the cover, it is important to add the oil through only one of the holes. The second hole allows air to escape, necessary for a smooth flow of liquid.

- Cut any solids that are to be processed into even-sized cubes of 2.5 cm (1 inch) for large processors and 1.5 cm (5/8 inch) for blenders and mini or small processors.

- Chopping or dicing meats is more successful if they are partially frozen. The blade will make clean cuts and the pieces will be of a uniform size.

- Where a recipe calls for dry ingredients such as flour to be sifted, they can be put directly into the processor bowl and whizzed for 3–5 seconds before adding the other ingredients. This will mix as well as aerate them, and will distribute them evenly over the base of the bowl.

- You will get better results when making pastry by using chilled butter.

- Use chilled cream for whisking.

- When using a whisking attachment for cream and egg whites, make sure that the processor bowl and the attachment are cleaned of all grease, and thoroughly dry.

- When chopping nuts such as pine nuts and walnuts that have a high oil content, add 1–2 teaspoons of a dry ingredient from the recipe (such as flour, cocoa, desiccated coconut), which will act as an absorbing agent and prevent the nuts becoming moist and oily.

- Always turn the machine off at the power point before removing any attachments and blades.

- Store metal blades as you would sharp knives — away from children but not tucked away where you're likely to inadvertently cut yourself.

- Processor bowls can be washed in the dishwasher, but they may cloud due to the alkaline content of your detergent.

- Clean coffee grinders and spice mills by wiping out the bowl with dry paper towels.

drinks

drink up

Perhaps the simplest of the whizzing repertoire, drinks are the perfect place to introduce a little colour and creativity. No need to wait for a special occasion — many of the ingredients will already be chilling out in your fridge or fruit bowl. And best of all, these drinks are so quick and easy that it's only a matter of minutes before you'll be proudly pouring your creation into a glass and sipping away. There's an inviting selection of thirst-quenchers, heart-warmers and sheer indulgences — juices, shakes, lassis and smoothies, as well as rich and creamy hot drinks. So whether it's summer, autumn, winter or spring, you're guaranteed to find something that's just your cup of tea.

lemon slush

serves 4

115 g (4 oz/1/2 cup) **caster (superfine) sugar**

1 small handful **mint**

3 **lemons**

400 ml (14 fl oz) **soda water (club soda)**

Bring 750 ml (26 fl oz/3 cups) of water to the boil in a heavy-based saucepan over medium–high heat. Add the sugar and mint, reduce the heat to low and simmer for 10 minutes, stirring constantly until the sugar has dissolved. Discard the mint, then set the syrup aside to cool.

Peel the lemons using a sharp knife, removing all the white pith. Cut the lemons into segments by cutting between the membranes. Put the lemon segments and cooled sugar syrup in a large metal or plastic mixing bowl. Using an immersion blender fitted with the chopping blade, whizz for 30 seconds, or until the lemon is reduced to a pulp. Strain the mixture through a fine sieve into a bowl, pressing down on the pulp to extract all the liquid. Discard the pulp. Transfer the mixture to the freezer for at least 3 hours, or until frozen.

Remove the mixture from the freezer and, using the immersion blender, whizz for 40 seconds, or until it resembles crushed ice. Spoon into four tall glasses and pour in the soda water. Stir to combine and serve immediately.

spanish hot chocolate

serves 4

500 ml (17 fl oz/2 cups) **milk**

4 cm x 3 cm (1½ x 1¼ inch) piece **orange zest**, white pith removed, lightly scored

250 g (9 oz/1⅔ cups) finely chopped good-quality **dark chocolate**

Put the milk and orange zest in a heavy-based saucepan. Bring to the boil over medium heat, stirring constantly. As soon as the milk comes to the boil, remove the pan from the heat and set aside to infuse for 5 minutes.

Discard the orange zest and return the milk to the stovetop over low heat. Add the chocolate and stir until the chocolate has melted, making sure that it doesn't stick to the bottom of the pan.

Using an immersion blender fitted with the blending or general purpose blade, whizz for 40 seconds, or until thick and frothy. Pour into four mugs or heatproof glasses and serve hot.

apricot eggnog

serves 4

1/2 **vanilla bean** or 1/2 teaspoon **natural vanilla extract**

120 g (41/4 oz/2/3 cup) **dried apricots**

1/2 **cinnamon stick**

600 ml (21 fl oz) **milk**

2 **eggs**

11/2 tablespoons **honey**

2 teaspoons **orange-flavoured liqueur**, or to taste

grated **nutmeg**, to serve

If using the vanilla bean, split the bean in half and scrape the seeds into a small saucepan. Add the vanilla bean, apricots, cinnamon stick and 150 ml (5 fl oz) of water and bring to the boil over medium heat. Reduce the heat and simmer for 5 minutes, or until the apricots are soft. Remove from the heat and cool slightly.

Discard the vanilla bean, if using, and cinnamon stick and transfer the mixture to a blender or processor fitted with the metal blade. Whizz for 15–20 seconds, or until smooth.

Add the milk, eggs, honey, liqueur and vanilla extract, if using, and whizz in short bursts until frothy. Divide among four mugs or heatproof glasses and sprinkle with grated nutmeg. Serve immediately.

tip The eggnog can also be chilled, then whizzed briefly until frothy just before serving.

Split the **vanilla bean** in half lengthways and scrape out the **seeds**.

Whizz the apricot mixture in a blender until smooth.

chocolate caramel thick shake

serves 4

2 x 60 g (2¹/4 oz) **caramel chocolate bars**, roughly chopped (see tip)

750 ml (26 fl oz/3 cups) **chocolate ice cream**

375 ml (13 fl oz/1¹/2 cups) **milk**

2 tablespoons **drinking chocolate powder**

Put the caramel bars and ice cream in a blender and whizz for 30 seconds, or until the caramel bars are finely chopped.

Add the milk and drinking chocolate powder and blend until thick and frothy. There will be some pieces of caramel bar left in the bottom of the blender.

Pour into four glasses. Spoon out the remaining pieces of caramel bar and divide among the glasses.

tip Use a caramel chocolate bar such as a Mars Bar or Moro. If unavailable, use your favourite caramel chocolate bar.

31

vietnamese shake

serves 4

1 large **mango**, about 400 g (14 oz)

2 **bananas**

200 g (7 oz/1½ cups) **ice cubes**

375 ml (13 fl oz/1½ cups) **milk**

125 ml (4 fl oz/½ cup) **condensed milk**

extra **ice cubes**, to serve

Prepare the mango by slicing off the cheeks with a sharp knife. Using a large spoon, scoop the flesh out of the skin. Cut the flesh into chunks and put it in a blender. Peel and roughly chop the bananas and add them to the blender.

Add the ice cubes and 125 ml (4 fl oz/½ cup) of the milk and whizz for 30 seconds, or until smooth. Add the remaining milk and the condensed milk and whizz for 15–20 seconds, or until frothy. Pour into four glasses and add the extra ice cubes.

tip This shake is best served immediately, but can be chilled and served within 30 minutes if preferred. If left any longer, the colour of the shake may be affected by the bananas.

tropical fruit shake

serves 4

185 ml (6 fl oz/3/4 cup) **guava nectar** or **guava juice**

2 tablespoons **lemon juice**

1 medium **yellow papaya**, about 650 g (1 lb 7 oz)

310 ml (103/4 fl oz/11/4 cups) **pineapple juice**

100 ml (31/2 fl oz) **milk**

2 small scoops **vanilla ice cream**

1–2 tablespoons **honey**, to taste

Combine the guava nectar or juice and lemon juice. Pour into ice cube trays and freeze until firm.

Peel the papaya and cut it into small cubes. Put the papaya in a blender with the pineapple juice, milk and ice cream and whizz for 25 seconds, or until smooth. Add the honey, to taste, and blend for 15–20 seconds, or until frothy.

Pour the shake into four glasses and divide the guava ice cubes among the glasses.

tip For a more refreshing shake, chill the papaya before use.

berry whizz

serves 4

250 g (9 oz/1²/3 cups) **strawberries**, hulled and chopped

150 g (5¹/2 oz/1 cup) fresh or frozen **blueberries**

185 g (6¹/2 oz/1¹/2 cups) fresh or frozen **raspberries**

625 ml (21¹/2 fl oz/2¹/2 cups) freshly squeezed **orange juice**

ice cubes (see tip, page 39)

1–2 tablespoons **caster (superfine) sugar**, to taste

mint leaves, to serve

Whizz the strawberries, blueberries and raspberries with some of the orange juice **until smooth**.

Push the **berry** mixture **through a sieve**, discarding the solids.

Put the strawberries, blueberries and raspberries in a blender with 250 ml (9 fl oz/ 1 cup) of the orange juice. Whizz for 35–45 seconds, or until smooth.

Use a large spoon to push the berry mixture through a sieve, discarding the solids.

Crush the ice in the blender (use the ice crusher button if the blender has one). Add the sieved berry purée, the remaining orange juice and the sugar, to taste. Whizz to combine, then taste for sweetness, adding more sugar if necessary.

Pour into four glasses and top each with a sprig of mint. Serve immediately.

tip Use 12 or more ice cubes if using fresh berries. If using frozen berries, you may prefer not to use ice cubes.

banana bender

serves 4

750 ml (26 fl oz/3 cups) **milk**

2 **bananas**

1 **egg**

2 tablespoons **malted milk powder**

1 tablespoon **honey**, optional

4 small scoops **vanilla ice cream**

extra **malted milk powder**, to serve

Put the milk in a covered container in the freezer for 30 minutes to make it very cold. It should be cold but not icy.

Peel and chop the bananas and put them in a blender. Add the milk, egg, malted milk powder and honey, if using. Whizz for 20 seconds, or until smooth.

Pour into four glasses, top each with a small scoop of ice cream and sprinkle with extra malted milk powder. Serve immediately.

tip Reduced-fat milk and ice cream can be used if preferred.

apricot smoothie

serves 4

500 ml (17 fl oz/2 cups) **milk**

420 g (15 oz) tin **apricots in light syrup**

200 g (7 oz/3/4 cup) **apricot yoghurt**

1 tablespoon **wheat germ** or **lecithin meal**

1/2 teaspoon **ground cinnamon**

honey, optional, to taste

extra **ground cinnamon**, to serve

Put the milk in a covered container in the freezer for 30 minutes to make it very cold. It should be cold but not icy.

Drain the apricots, then put them in a blender. Add the milk, yoghurt, wheat germ or lecithin meal, and cinnamon. Whizz for 30 seconds, or until smooth. Sweeten with honey, if using.

Pour into four glasses and sprinkle with a little extra cinnamon. Serve immediately.

tips Low-fat milk and yoghurt can be used if preferred. For a more refreshing smoothie, chill the apricots before use.

summer fruit soy smoothie

serves 4

1 **banana**

4 **peaches**, chopped

175 g (6 oz/3/4 cup) **apricot and mango soy yoghurt** or **vanilla soy yoghurt**

1 tablespoon **lecithin meal**

1 teaspoon **natural vanilla extract**

625 ml (21 1/2 fl oz/2 1/2 cups) **plain soy milk** or **vanilla soy milk**

1 tablespoon **maple syrup**, optional

extra **peach** slices, to serve

ice cubes, to serve

Put the banana, peach, yoghurt, lecithin meal, vanilla extract and 250 ml (9 fl oz/ 1 cup) of the soy milk in a blender. Whizz for 30 seconds, or until smooth.

Add the remaining soy milk and whizz for a further 30 seconds, or until combined. Taste for sweetness and add the maple syrup, if using. Put the ice and extra peach slices in four glasses, pour in the smoothie and serve immediately.

tips Use fat-free soy milk and yoghurt if preferred. If fresh peaches are not available, use 4 tinned peach halves.

rich mocha warmer

serves 4

200 ml (7 fl oz) freshly brewed strong **espresso coffee**

50 g (13/4 oz/1/3 cup) roughly chopped good-quality **dark chocolate**

500 ml (17 fl oz/2 cups) **milk**

raw or golden caster (superfine) sugar, to taste

whipped cream, to serve

4 **cinnamon sticks**, to serve

chocolate-coated coffee beans, optional, to serve

grated **nutmeg**, to serve

Put the hot coffee and chocolate in a 1 litre (35 fl oz/4 cup) heatproof pitcher and set aside for 1–1 1/2 minutes until the chocolate has melted, stirring once or twice.

Meanwhile, put the milk in a small saucepan and gently heat over low heat to just below boiling point. Pour the milk into the pitcher containing the coffee mixture. Using an immersion blender fitted with the blending or general purpose blade, whizz for 30–45 seconds, or until smooth and frothy. Add the sugar, to taste.

Pour into four warmed mugs or latte glasses and top each with a scoop of whipped cream. Add the cinnamon sticks and chocolate-coated coffee beans, if using. Sprinkle with nutmeg and serve immediately.

Combine the hot **coffee** and chocolate and set aside until the **chocolate** has melted.

Pour the **hot milk** into the pitcher with the coffee and chocolate **mixture**.

raspberry and banana low-fat smoothie

serves 4

625 ml (21 1/2 fl oz/2 1/2 cups) **low-fat milk**

2 **bananas**

125 g (4 1/2 oz/1 cup) fresh or frozen **raspberries**

200 g (7 oz/3/4 cup) **low-fat vanilla yoghurt**

1 tablespoon **oat bran** or **lecithin meal**

Put the milk in a covered container in the freezer for 30 minutes to make it very cold. It should be cold but not icy.

Peel and chop the bananas and put them in a blender. Add the raspberries, yoghurt, oat bran or lecithin meal, and 250 ml (9 fl oz/1 cup) of the milk. Whizz for 30 seconds, or until smooth.

Add the remaining milk and whizz for a further 30 seconds, or until combined. Pour into four glasses and serve immediately.

tip Add 1 tablespoon of honey for sweetness, if desired.

mango lassi

serves 4

2 large **mangoes**, about 400 g (14 oz) each

500 g (1 lb 2 oz/2 cups) **Greek-style yoghurt**

2 teaspoons **lemon juice**

3–4 tablespoons **caster (superfine) sugar**, to taste

ice cubes, optional, to serve

extra diced **mango**, to serve

Prepare the mangoes by slicing off the cheeks with a sharp knife. Using a large spoon, scoop the flesh out of the skin. Cut the flesh into chunks and put it in a blender with the yoghurt, lemon juice and 3 tablespoons of the sugar.

Add 185 ml (6 fl oz/3/4 cup) of cold water and whizz for 40–60 seconds, or until smooth. Taste for sweetness and add extra sugar, if desired.

Put some ice cubes, if using, in the bottom of four glasses. Pour the lassi over the top and serve immediately, topped with diced mango.

coconut and lychee lassi

serves 4

565 g (1 lb 4 oz) tin **lychees in syrup**

270 ml (9 1/2 fl oz) **coconut milk**

115 g (4 oz/1/2 cup) **caster (superfine) sugar**

1 **lemon grass stem**, white part only, bruised

grated **zest** and **juice** of 1 **lime**

200 g (7 oz/3/4 cup) **plain yoghurt**

1 teaspoon **dried basil seeds**, optional (see tip, page 56)

lime wedges, to serve

Drain the lychees, reserving 150 ml (5 fl oz) of the syrup as well as the lychees. Put the syrup in a saucepan and add the coconut milk, sugar, lemon grass and lime zest. Stir over medium heat until the sugar has dissolved. Bring to the boil, then reduce the heat and simmer for 1 minute. Remove from the heat and set aside to infuse for 15 minutes.

Strain the mixture into a blender and add the reserved lychees and yoghurt. Whizz for 30 seconds, or until smooth. Add the lime juice and whizz until just combined. Refrigerate until very cold.

When ready to serve, put the basil seeds, if using, in a small bowl and cover with water. Set aside for 3–4 minutes, or until the seeds have swelled. Stir the lassi, then pour into four glasses and top with the basil seeds. Serve with lime wedges, if desired.

tip Dried basil seeds are available from Asian supermarkets. When soaked in water they swell and become gelatinous. They add texture to the drink but no flavour.

Combine the lychee syrup, coconut milk, **sugar**, lemon grass and lime zest in a saucepan.

Strain the mixture into a **blender** and add the lychees and **yoghurt**.

almond and nectarine milk

serves 4

125 g (4¹/2 oz/³/4 cup) **blanched almonds**

6 **nectarines**, peeled and chopped

115 g (4 oz/¹/2 cup) **caster (superfine) sugar**

¹/2 teaspoon **lemon juice**

grated **nutmeg**, to serve

Put the almonds in a bowl and cover with plenty of cold water. Soak overnight. Drain, then rinse and discard any nuts with blemishes.

Put the almonds in a blender or small processor fitted with the metal blade, add 150 ml (5 fl oz) of cold water and whizz for 25 seconds, or until smooth. Add another 250 ml (9 fl oz/1 cup) of cold water and whizz for 30–35 seconds. Set aside for 2 hours.

Strain the almond mixture into a bowl through muslin or a fine sieve, squeezing to extract the liquid. Discard the solids.

Wipe out the blender or processor with paper towels and add the nectarines and sugar. Whizz for 20 seconds, or until smooth, then add the almond milk and lemon juice. With the motor running, gradually pour in 125 ml (4 fl oz/¹/2 cup) of cold water; chill.

When ready to serve, pour into four glasses and dust with nutmeg.

energy fruit smoothie

serves 4

1/2 (about 650 g/1 lb 7 oz) **rockmelon** or **any orange-fleshed melon**

1 **mango**

2 tablespoons **toasted muesli**

1 tablespoon **honey**

1 tablespoon **malted milk powder**

100 g (31/2 oz/1/3 cup) **Greek-style apricot yoghurt**

125 ml (4 fl oz/1/2 cup) **orange juice**

250 ml (9 fl oz/1 cup) **skim milk**

Peel the melon, scoop out the seeds and roughly chop the flesh. Prepare the mango by slicing off the cheeks with a sharp knife. Using a large spoon, scoop the flesh out of the skin. Cut the flesh into chunks.

Put the melon, mango and toasted muesli in a blender and whizz for 20 seconds, or until smooth. Add the honey, malted milk powder and yoghurt and whizz for 10 seconds. Add the orange juice and skim milk and whizz for 30 seconds, or until foaming. Pour into four glasses to serve.

tip The fruit may be chilled beforehand for a colder drink, or the smoothie can be chilled for up to 2 hours before serving.

summer egg flip

serves 4

4 **apricots**

2 large **yellow peaches**

2 tablespoons **maple syrup**

125 g (4¹/2 oz/¹/2 cup) **berry yoghurt**

600 ml (21 fl oz) **milk**

2 **eggs**

whizz it

Prepare the apricots and peaches by carefully removing the skin and roughly chopping the flesh.

Put the apricots, peaches, maple syrup, yoghurt, milk and eggs in a blender and whizz for 30 seconds, or until smooth. Continue whizzing for 20 seconds, or until foaming. Pour into four large glasses and serve immediately.

tip If apricots and peaches are out of season, use tinned apricots and peaches instead.

Carefully **peel** the apricots and peaches before **chopping** the flesh.

Combine the **apricots**, peaches, maple syrup, yoghurt, milk and **eggs** in a blender.

watermelon, pineapple and ginger cooler

serves 4

1 kg (2 lb 4 oz) **seedless watermelon**

4 cm (1 1/2 inch) piece young **ginger**

250 ml (9 fl oz/1 cup) **pineapple juice**, chilled

250 ml (9 fl oz/1 cup) **tropical fruit juice**, chilled

ice cubes, to serve

Remove the skin from the watermelon and cut the flesh into large chunks. Peel and finely grate the ginger.

Put the watermelon and ginger in a blender and whizz for 20–25 seconds, or until smooth. With the motor running, add the pineapple and tropical fruit juices and whizz until combined.

Pour into four glasses and top with ice cubes. Stir briskly and serve immediately.

tips If preferred, the watermelon may be chilled after being skinned and cut into chunks. Any tropical juice such as guava, mango or mixed fruit can be used.

double strawberry thick shake

serves 4

250 g (9 oz/1²/3 cups) **strawberries**

4 scoops **strawberry ice cream**

2 tablespoons **malted milk powder**

375 ml (13 fl oz/1¹/2 cups) **milk**

extra **malted milk powder**, to serve

Select two small strawberries for garnishing and halve them from top to bottom, cutting through the hull. Without slicing all the way through, cut each half from bottom to top into two slices joined at the stalk. Gently fan out the slices; reserve.

Hull the remaining strawberries and cut them in half, removing the white core if it is pronounced. Put the strawberries, ice cream and malted milk powder in a blender and whizz for 20–25 seconds, or until thick and smooth.

Add the milk and whizz for 25–30 seconds, or until frothy. Pour into four glasses and top each with one of the reserved strawberry halves. Sprinkle with extra malted milk powder. Serve immediately.

lime and ruby grapefruit soda

serves 4

4 **limes**

1 **ruby grapefruit**

350 ml (12 fl oz) **lime juice cordial**

1 litre (35 fl oz/4 cups) **soda water (club soda),** chilled

Peel two of the limes using a sharp knife, removing all the white pith. Discard the peel and pith. Cut the peeled limes into segments by cutting between the membranes. Put each lime segment into a hole of an ice cube tray, cover with water and freeze until firm.

Peel the remaining limes and the grapefruit, removing all the white pith. Discard the peel and pith. Put the fruit in a blender or small processor fitted with the metal blade and whizz for 25–45 seconds, or until puréed. Strain into a large pitcher through a coarse sieve; some texture is desirable.

Just before serving, add the lime juice cordial and soda water. Pour into four tall glasses and add the lime ice cubes.

tip The sieved juice can be made up to 24 hours in advance and stored, covered, in the refrigerator.

soups

slurp away

If smooth and creamy is your idea of the perfect soup, you'll be right at home with this delicious collection. But if thick and chunky is more your style, there's something here for you too. Vegetables come into their own in the soup bowl, but we've also invited noodles, lentils, beans, meat, seafood and herbs to join the party. From light and breezy cool summer openers to thick one-pot meals for wintry weather, these recipe shows just how easy it is to create colourful crowd-pleasers with an exciting blend of flavours and textures. No one will guess that you've spent only minutes slaving over a hot processor.

roasted leek and celeriac soup

serves 4

2 tablespoons **olive oil**

800 g (1 lb 12 oz/about 2 large) **leeks**,
  white part only, cut into 5 cm
  (2 inch) lengths

1 **garlic bulb**, unpeeled, halved

800 g (1 lb 12 oz/1 medium) **celeriac**,
  chopped

250 ml (9 fl oz/1 cup) **milk**

125 ml (4 fl oz/1/2 cup) **thick
  (double/heavy) cream**

2 tablespoons snipped **chives**

slices of toasted **baguette**, to serve

Preheat the oven to 200°C (400°F/Gas 6). Put the olive oil in a roasting tin and heat in the oven for 5 minutes. Add the leek and garlic bulb halves and season with salt and freshly ground black pepper. Shake the roasting tin to coat the vegetables with the oil. Roast for 20–25 minutes, or until the leek is tender. Remove the leek and roast the garlic for a further 10–15 minutes, or until tender when pierced with the tip of a knife.

Meanwhile, put the celeriac and 750 ml (26 fl oz/3 cups) of water in a large saucepan. Cover and bring to the boil, then reduce the heat to medium–low and simmer for 20 minutes, or until tender. Add the roasted leek.

Squeeze or scoop the garlic into the saucepan. Season with salt and freshly ground black pepper and mix well. Add the milk.

Remove the saucepan from the heat. Using an immersion blender fitted with the chopping blade, whizz for 45 seconds, or until puréed. Stir through the cream and gently reheat the soup. Check the seasoning and thickness, adding additional milk if the soup is too thick. Sprinkle with the chives and serve topped with slices of toasted baguette.

cauliflower, cannellini bean and prosciutto soup

serves 4

2 tablespoons **olive oil**

100 g (3¹/2 oz/about 8 slices) **prosciutto**, chopped

1 **onion**, chopped

1 **garlic clove**, minced

800 g (1 lb 12 oz) **cauliflower**, cut into small florets

2 x 400 g (14 oz) tins **cannellini beans**, drained

125 ml (4 fl oz/¹/2 cup) **thick (double/heavy) cream**

snipped **chives**, to serve

Heat 1 tablespoon of the oil in a large saucepan over medium–high heat. Add the prosciutto and fry, stirring often, until crisp. Transfer half the prosciutto to a plate lined with paper towel, leaving the rest in the saucepan.

Reduce the heat to medium. Add the remaining oil and the onion to the saucepan and fry for 5 minutes, or until softened. Add the garlic and cauliflower florets and fry for 3 minutes.

Add the cannellini beans and 1 litre (35 fl oz/4 cups) of water and season well with salt and freshly ground black pepper. Bring to the boil, then reduce the heat and simmer, covered, for 15 minutes, or until the cauliflower is tender. Set aside to cool for 10 minutes.

Using an immersion blender fitted with the chopping blade, whizz the soup for 25 seconds, or until smooth. Season with salt and plenty of freshly ground black pepper. Stir through the cream and gently reheat the soup. Serve immediately, with the reserved crisp prosciutto and the chives sprinkled on top.

vietnamese pork and prawn ball soup with cellophane noodles

serves 4

pork and prawn balls

2 **garlic cloves**, roughly chopped

1 **lemon grass stem**, white part only, sliced

300 g (10$^{1}/_{2}$ oz) **pork spareribs**, skin and bones removed,
  cut into chunks (see tip, page 82)

125 g (4$^{1}/_{2}$ oz) **raw king prawns (shrimp)**, peeled and deveined

1 small handful **coriander (cilantro) leaves**

2 teaspoons **fish sauce**

1.5 litres (52 fl oz/6 cups) **chicken stock**

1 **lemon grass stem**, white part only, sliced

1 small **red chilli**, sliced (seeded if preferred)

8 **raw prawns (shrimp)**, peeled and deveined, leaving the tails intact

100 g (3$^{1}/_{2}$ oz) **bean vermicelli noodles (cellophane noodles)**

1–2 teaspoons **fish sauce**, to taste

60 ml (2 fl oz/$^{1}/_{4}$ cup) **lime juice**

90 g (3$^{1}/_{4}$ oz/1 cup) **bean sprouts**, trimmed

1 handful **Vietnamese mint**, to serve

1 handful **coriander (cilantro) leaves**, to serve

To make the pork and prawn balls, put the garlic, lemon grass and pork in a small processor fitted with the metal blade and whizz for 20–35 seconds, or until finely chopped, occasionally scraping down the side of the processor bowl. Add the prawns, coriander and fish sauce and whizz in short bursts until the prawns are chopped but still large enough to give the balls some texture. Using moistened hands, roll 2 teaspoons of mixture at a time into small balls.

Heat the stock in a saucepan, add the lemon grass and chilli and bring to the boil. Add the pork and prawn balls and simmer for 5 minutes. Add the prawns and noodles and simmer over low heat for 1–2 minutes, or until the prawns have a tinge of orange and are almost cooked. Add the fish sauce, to taste, and lime juice.

Ladle the soup into four bowls and serve the bean sprouts, Vietnamese mint and coriander on top.

tip Use pork spareribs with good layers of meat and fat.

Add the prawns, coriander and fish sauce to the chopped **pork mixture**.

Put the **stock**, lemon grass and chilli in a saucepan and bring **to the boil**.

spiced pumpkin and lentil soup

serves 4

1 kg (2 lb 4 oz) **pumpkin (squash)**

2 tablespoons **olive oil**

1 large **onion**, chopped

3 **garlic cloves**, chopped

1 teaspoon **ground turmeric**

1/2 teaspoon **ground coriander**

1/2 teaspoon **ground cumin**

1/2 teaspoon **chilli flakes**

135 g (43/4 oz/1/2 cup) **red lentils**, rinsed and drained

1 litre (35 fl oz/4 cups) **boiling water**

90 g (31/4 oz/1/3 cup) **plain yoghurt**, to serve

Peel, seed and cube the pumpkin to give 700 g (1 lb 9 oz/41/2 cups) of flesh.

Heat the oil in a large saucepan over medium heat. Add the onion and garlic and fry for 5 minutes, or until softened, being careful not to burn the garlic. Add the turmeric, coriander, cumin and chilli flakes and fry, stirring constantly, for 2 minutes.

Add the pumpkin, red lentils and boiling water. Bring to the boil, then reduce the heat and simmer, covered, for 20 minutes, or until the pumpkin and lentils are tender. Set aside to cool for 5 minutes.

Using an immersion blender fitted with the chopping blade, whizz the soup for 25–35 seconds, or until evenly chopped. Season well with salt and freshly ground black pepper and reheat the soup.

Ladle the soup into four bowls, top with a spoonful of the yoghurt and sprinkle with freshly ground black pepper.

ham and pea soup

serves 4

2 tablespoons **olive oil**

1 large **onion**, chopped

3 **celery stalks**, sliced

about 40 **sage leaves**

220 g (73/4 oz/1 cup) **green split peas**, rinsed and drained

1 **smoked ham hock**, about 800 g (1 lb 12 oz)

1 **thyme sprig**

vegetable oil, for pan-frying

Heat the oil in a large saucepan over medium heat. Add the onion, celery and four of the sage leaves and fry, stirring often, for 5 minutes, or until the onion and celery are soft.

Add the green split peas, ham hock, thyme sprig and 1.25 litres (44 fl oz/5 cups) of water. Bring to the boil, then reduce the heat, cover and simmer for 11/2 hours, or until the meat is falling off the bone.

Remove the saucepan from the heat and discard the thyme sprig. Remove the ham hock from the saucepan and, when cool enough to handle, cut off the meat and return it to the soup. Discard the bone. Using an immersion blender fitted with the chopping blade, whizz the soup for 30 seconds, or until smooth. Season with freshly ground black pepper, and salt if necessary – the ham may be quite salty.

Pour the vegetable oil into a small saucepan to a depth of 3 cm (11/4 inches) and heat over high heat. Very carefully add the remaining sage leaves (standing back as they may spit) and fry for a few seconds, or until they turn bright green and become crisp. Remove quickly using a slotted spoon and drain on paper towel.

Gently reheat the soup and ladle into four bowls. Sprinkle the fried sage leaves on top of the soup. Serve with crispbread.

tip Smoked ham hocks are available from butchers and some delicatessens.

watercress, leek and potato soup

serves 4

350 g (12 oz) **watercress**, trimmed

1 tablespoon **oil**

1 **leek**, white part only, chopped

2 **garlic cloves**, chopped

1 **celery stalk**, chopped

1 teaspoon freshly grated **nutmeg**

500 g (1 lb 2 oz/4 medium) **potatoes**, chopped

1 litre (35 fl oz/4 cups) **chicken stock** or **vegetable stock**

250 ml (9 fl oz/1 cup) **milk**

1 handful **mint**

Reserve a few watercress leaves for serving. Pick off the remaining leaves in bunches, discarding the thick stems. Roughly chop and reserve the watercress.

Heat the oil in a large heavy-based saucepan. Add the leek, garlic and celery. Stir for 2 minutes to coat the vegetables in the oil. Reduce the heat, cover and simmer, stirring occasionally, for 5 minutes. Do not allow the vegetables to brown.

Add the nutmeg, potato and stock. Slowly bring to the boil, then reduce the heat and simmer, covered, for 20 minutes. Stir in the chopped watercress. Set aside to cool for 10 minutes.

Stir the milk and mint into the soup. Using an immersion blender fitted with the chopping blade, whizz for 1 minute, or until puréed to the desired consistency.

Gently reheat the soup and season well with salt and freshly ground black pepper. Ladle into bowls and garnish with the reserved watercress leaves.

tip The soup will keep in the refrigerator, covered, for up to 4 days, or in an airtight container in the freezer for up to 1 month.

borlotti bean and italian sausage soup

serves 4

2 tablespoons **olive oil**

3 thin **Italian sausages**

100 g (31/2 oz) thickly sliced **pancetta**, cut into 5 mm x 2 cm
  (1/4 inch x 3/4 inch) strips

2 **onions**, chopped

1 **leek**, white part only, sliced

2 **garlic cloves**, chopped

2 **celery stalks**, chopped

2 **carrots**, chopped

2 large **thyme sprigs**

1 litre (35 fl oz/4 cups) **chicken stock** or **vegetable stock**

400 g (14 oz) tin **borlotti (cranberry) beans**, rinsed and drained

410 g (141/2 oz) tin **diced tomatoes**

2 large handfuls **flat-leaf (Italian) parsley**, chopped

Add the **pancetta** halfway through browning the **sausages**.

Use an immersion blender to **whizz** the soup until it is roughly **puréed**.

Heat a little of the oil in a large frying pan over medium heat. Fry the sausages for 5–6 minutes, or until browned all over. Add the pancetta halfway through cooking. Remove from the heat and set aside.

Heat the remaining oil in a large heavy-based saucepan and add the onion, leek, garlic, celery and carrot. Stir for 2 minutes to coat the vegetables in the oil. Reduce the heat, cover and simmer, stirring occasionally, for 10 minutes. Do not allow the vegetables to brown.

Add the thyme sprigs and stock. Slowly bring to the boil, then reduce the heat and simmer, covered, for 20 minutes. Add the beans and remove the thyme sprigs. Remove the saucepan from the heat.

Using an immersion blender fitted with the chopping blade, whizz for 30 seconds, or until the soup is roughly puréed but still has some texture.

Dice the sausages and add them to the soup along with the pancetta and diced tomatoes. Gently reheat the soup. Stir through the parsley and season with plenty of salt and freshly ground black pepper.

tips If you prefer a chunkier texture, only purée half of the soup. The soup will keep in the refrigerator, covered, for up to 5 days, or in an airtight container in the freezer for up to 1 month.

zucchini and basil soup

serves 4

1 large **onion**, finely chopped

3 **garlic cloves**, very finely chopped

1/2 teaspoon **coriander seeds**

2 **celery stalks**, finely diced

6 **zucchini (courgettes)**, roughly diced

3 large **waxy potatoes**, diced

1.25 litres (44 fl oz/5 cups) **chicken stock**

125 g (41/2 oz/1/2 cup) **crème fraîche** or **sour cream**

1 large handful **basil**, torn

2 tablespoons finely chopped **flat-leaf (Italian) parsley**

sea salt, to serve

Put the onion, garlic, coriander seeds, celery, zucchini, potato and stock in a large heavy-based saucepan. Bring to the boil over medium heat. Partially cover the saucepan and gently simmer for 12–15 minutes, or until all the vegetables are cooked through.

Meanwhile, put the crème fraîche or sour cream in a small bowl with half the basil and the parsley. Mix together using a fork, then set aside.

Remove the saucepan from the heat. Using an immersion blender fitted with the chopping blade, whizz the soup for 20 seconds, or until it is semi-smooth. Stir in the remaining basil. Season with salt and freshly ground black pepper, to taste.

Divide the crème fraîche mixture among four bowls, ladle the soup into the bowls and sprinkle with sea salt and freshly ground black pepper. Serve immediately.

creamy brussels sprout and leek soup

serves 4

1 tablespoon **olive oil**

2 **rindless bacon slices**, chopped

2 **garlic cloves**, chopped

3 **leeks**, white part only, sliced

300 g (10½ oz) **brussels sprouts**, roughly chopped

750 ml (26 fl oz/3 cups) **chicken stock** or **vegetable stock**

185 ml (6 fl oz/¾ cup) **pouring cream** or **milk**

slices of toasted **crusty bread**, to serve

Heat the oil in a large saucepan over medium heat. Add the chopped bacon and fry for 3 minutes. Add the garlic and leek, cover and fry, stirring often, for a further 5 minutes. Add the brussels sprouts, stir to combine, cover and cook, stirring often, for 5 minutes.

Add the stock and season with salt and freshly ground black pepper. Bring to the boil, then reduce the heat, cover the pan and simmer for 10 minutes, or until the vegetables are very tender. Set aside to cool for 10 minutes.

Using an immersion blender fitted with the chopping blade, whizz the soup for 25–30 seconds, or until puréed. Stir through the cream or milk and gently reheat the soup. Serve with slices of toasted crusty bread.

tip For a vegetarian version of this soup, simply omit the bacon and use vegetable stock rather than chicken stock.

beetroot and red capsicum soup

serves 4

6 medium **beetroot (beets)**, 600 g (1 lb 5 oz) without stems and leaves

1 tablespoon **oil**

1 **red onion**, chopped

1 **celery stalk**, chopped

1 **garlic clove**, chopped

1 large **red capsicum (pepper)**, seeded and chopped

410 g (14 1/2 oz) tin **chopped tomatoes**

1 tablespoon **red wine vinegar**

sour cream, to serve

2 tablespoons finely snipped **chives**, to serve

Wearing protective gloves, peel the beetroot with a vegetable peeler and cut it into 3 cm (1 1/4 inch) dice. Put the beetroot in a large saucepan with 1 litre (35 fl oz/ 4 cups) of water. Slowly bring to the boil over medium–low heat, then reduce the heat and simmer for 25–30 minutes, or until the beetroot is tender when pierced with a fork. Remove about 1/2 cup of beetroot cubes, dice finely and set aside.

Meanwhile, heat the oil in a large heavy-based saucepan over medium heat. Add the onion, celery, garlic and capsicum and stir to coat the vegetables in the oil. Reduce the heat to low, cover and cook, stirring occasionally, for 10 minutes. Do not allow the vegetables to brown. Add the chopped tomatoes and vinegar and simmer for 10 minutes.

Transfer the tomato mixture to the saucepan containing the beetroot and remove the pan from the heat. Using an immersion blender fitted with the chopping blade, whizz the soup for 20–30 seconds, or until smooth. Season well with salt and freshly ground black pepper.

Ladle the soup into four warm bowls and top with a spoonful of sour cream, the reserved diced beetroot and the chives.

tip The soup will keep in the refrigerator, covered, for up to 4 days, or in an airtight container in the freezer for up to 1 month.

alsace mushroom soup

serves 4

10 g (1/4 oz) **dried porcini mushrooms**

250 ml (9 fl oz/1 cup) **hot water**

50 g (13/4 oz) **butter**

1 **onion**, roughly chopped

4 **French shallots**, chopped

1 large **potato**, about 185 g (61/2 oz), chopped

1 **celery stalk**, chopped

2 **garlic cloves**, chopped

1 small **red chilli**, seeded and chopped

175 g (6 oz) **flat mushrooms**, roughly chopped

175 g (6 oz) **Swiss brown mushrooms**, roughly chopped

750 ml (26 fl oz/3 cups) **chicken stock** or **vegetable stock**

2 large **thyme sprigs**

1–2 teaspoons **lemon juice**, to taste

90 g (31/4 oz/1/3 cup) **sour cream**, to serve

2 tablespoons finely chopped **flat-leaf (Italian) parsley**, to serve

1 tablespoon grated **lemon zest**, to serve

Put the porcini mushrooms in a small bowl and pour over the hot water. Set aside to soften for 10 minutes.

Meanwhile, heat the butter in a large heavy-based saucepan. Add the onion, shallots, potato, celery, garlic and chilli. Stir for 2 minutes to coat the vegetables in the butter. Reduce the heat, cover and simmer, stirring occasionally, for 5 minutes. Do not allow the vegetables to brown.

Add the fresh mushrooms to the saucepan and cook, stirring, for 2–3 minutes. Add the stock, thyme sprigs and porcini mushrooms with their soaking water. Slowly bring to the boil over low heat, then reduce the heat and simmer, covered, for 15 minutes. Discard the thyme sprigs. Set aside to cool slightly.

Using an immersion blender fitted with the chopping blade, whizz the soup for 15–20 seconds, or until roughly puréed. The soup should still have texture. Add the lemon juice, to taste, and season well with salt and freshly ground black pepper.

Gently reheat the soup and ladle into warm bowls. Top with a spoonful of the sour cream and sprinkle with the parsley and lemon zest.

tip The soup will keep in the refrigerator, covered, for up to 4 days, or in an airtight container in the freezer for up to 1 month.

Peel and roughly chop **the onion**.

Soak the porcini mushrooms in hot water until the **mushrooms** are soft.

smoked fish chowder

serves 4–6

500 ml (17 fl oz/2 cups) **milk**

500 g (1 lb 2 oz) **smoked fish**, trimmed
and cut into large chunks

50 g (1 3/4 oz) **butter**

1 **leek**, white part only, roughly
chopped

2 **celery stalks**, chopped

1 large **carrot**, chopped

2 **garlic cloves**, chopped

400 g (14 oz/3 medium) **potatoes**, cut
into 5 cm (2 inch) pieces

1 teaspoon freshly grated **nutmeg**

500 ml (17 fl oz/2 cups) **chicken stock**
or **fish stock**

125 ml (4 fl oz/1/2 cup) **pouring cream**

1 large handful **flat-leaf (Italian)**
parsley, chopped

Heat the milk in a large deep saucepan. Add the fish and simmer for 8 minutes, or until the flesh flakes when tested. Transfer the fish to a plate and set aside to cool. Reserve the milk. Peel and discard the skin from the fish and roughly flake the flesh, removing any bones.

Heat the butter in a large heavy-based saucepan over medium–low heat. Add the leek, celery, carrot and garlic. Stir for 2 minutes to coat the vegetables in the butter. Reduce the heat, cover and sweat, stirring occasionally, for 5 minutes. Do not allow the vegetables to brown.

Add the chopped potato and nutmeg to the saucepan and stir to combine. Cook for 2 minutes, then add the stock. Bring to the boil, cover and cook for 20 minutes, or until the potato is tender. Set aside to cool slightly.

Using an immersion blender fitted with the chopping blade, whizz the soup for 10 seconds, or until roughly puréed. Stir in the fish, reserved milk, cream and parsley and gently reheat the soup. Season well with freshly ground black pepper.

tip The soup will keep in the refrigerator, covered, for up to 3 days. It is not suitable for freezing.

panzanella

serves 4

1 **green capsicum (pepper)**, halved
  and seeded

1 **Lebanese (short) cucumber**, peeled,
  halved and seeded

1/2 small **red onion**

1 **celery stalk**

1–2 **garlic cloves**

410 g (14 1/2 oz) tin **chopped tomatoes**

2 tablespoons **tomato paste**
  (concentrated purée)

250 ml (9 fl oz/1 cup) **tomato passata**
  (puréed tomatoes)

1 1/2 tablespoons **white wine vinegar**

1 tablespoon **olive oil**

1 teaspoon **soft brown sugar**

100 g (3 1/2 oz) stale **country-style white
  bread**, crusts removed

2 tablespoons sliced **black olives**, to
  serve

2 tablespoons **baby capers**, rinsed and
  squeezed dry, to serve

2 tablespoons chopped **flat-leaf
  (Italian) parsley**, to serve

Roughly chop the capsicum, cucumber, red onion, celery and garlic. Combine in a large processor fitted with the metal blade and add the chopped tomatoes and tomato paste. Whizz for 30 seconds, or until smooth.

Add 250 ml (9 fl oz/1 cup) water, the tomato passata, vinegar, oil and brown sugar. Season well with salt and freshly ground black pepper. Whizz in 3-second bursts for 20 seconds, or until well combined. Transfer the mixture to a bowl.

Preheat the grill (broiler) to medium. Tear the bread into 2 cm (3/4 inch) chunks, put on a baking tray and toast under the grill until crisp but not browned. Stir the bread through the tomato mixture. Set aside for 15 minutes to allow the flavours to develop. Serve in four bowls topped with the olives, capers and parsley.

tip The soup, without the bread, will keep in the refrigerator, covered, for up to 3 days. It is not suitable for freezing.

spicy corn and coconut soup

serves 4

1 tablespoon **oil**

1 large **onion**, chopped

1 **celery stalk**, chopped

2 **garlic cloves**, chopped

1 teaspoon **ground coriander**

1½ teaspoons **ground cumin**

1–2 teaspoons **sambal oelek** (see tip)

500 g (1 lb 2 oz) **potatoes**, chopped

750 ml (26 fl oz/3 cups) **chicken stock**

or **vegetable stock**

420 g (14¾ oz) tin **corn kernels,**

drained

270 ml (9½ fl oz) **light coconut milk**

1 handful **coriander (cilantro) leaves**

310 g (11 oz) tin **creamed corn**

extra **coriander leaves**, to serve

Heat the oil in a large heavy-based saucepan over medium–low heat. Add the onion, celery and garlic. Stir for 2 minutes to coat the vegetables in the oil. Reduce the heat, cover and simmer, stirring occasionally, for 5 minutes. Do not allow the vegetables to brown.

Add the ground coriander, cumin and 1 teaspoon of the sambal oelek and stir for 1 minute. Add the potato and stock. Bring slowly to the boil, then reduce the heat and simmer, covered, for 15 minutes, or until the potato is cooked. Stir in the corn kernels, coconut milk and coriander leaves. Set aside to cool slightly.

Using an immersion blender fitted with the chopping blade, whizz the soup for 20–30 seconds, or until smooth. Stir in the creamed corn and gently reheat the soup. Add a little hot water if you prefer a thinner consistency. Season well with salt and freshly ground black pepper. Ladle into four warm bowls and add the remaining sambal oelek, to taste. Sprinkle with the extra coriander leaves.

tip Sambal oelek is a fiery condiment used in Malaysian, Indonesian and Singaporean cuisines. It is made from red chillies, vinegar and sugar and is available in jars from Asian supermarkets.

chilled cucumber yoghurt soup

serves 4

2 **telegraph (long) cucumbers**, about 550 g (1 lb 4 oz)

1 large handful **mint**

2 **garlic cloves**, chopped

1 teaspoon **dried mint**

125 ml (4 fl oz/1/2 cup) **milk**

500 g (1 lb 2 oz/2 cups) **Greek-style yoghurt**

2–3 teaspoons **lemon juice**, to taste

3–4 drops **Tabasco sauce**, to taste

2 tablespoons finely snipped **chives**, to serve

Peel the cucumbers, halve them lengthways and scoop out the seeds. Set aside about one-third of one of the cucumbers.

Put the remaining cucumber in a small processor fitted with the metal blade. Add the mint, garlic, dried mint and milk and whizz in 3–4 second bursts for 20 seconds. Add the yoghurt, and the lemon juice and Tabasco sauce to taste, and season well with salt and freshly ground black pepper. Whizz until well combined and smooth. Transfer the soup to a bowl, cover and refrigerate for at least 2 hours to allow the flavours to develop.

Finely dice the reserved cucumber. Ladle the soup into bowls and top with the diced cucumber and chives.

tip The soup should be consumed within 1 day. It is not suitable for freezing.

potato and anchovy chowder with garlic prawns

serves 4

garlic prawns

2 **garlic cloves**, chopped

1 small **red chilli**, seeded and chopped

2 tablespoons chopped **flat-leaf (Italian) parsley**

1 tablespoon **olive oil**

16 **raw prawns (shrimp)**, peeled and deveined

1 tablespoon **olive oil**

3 **bacon slices**, fat trimmed, chopped

1 **onion**, chopped

2 **celery stalks**, chopped

2 **garlic cloves**, chopped

80 g (2¾ oz) tin **anchovies**, drained

1 **carrot**, chopped

3 **potatoes**, about 400 g (14 oz), roughly chopped

375 ml (13 fl oz/1½ cups) **chicken stock** or **fish stock**

250 ml (9 fl oz/1 cup) **milk**

125 ml (4 fl oz/½ cup) **pouring cream**

3 tablespoons finely chopped **flat-leaf (Italian) parsley**

To make the garlic prawns, put the garlic, chilli and parsley in a mini processor and whizz for 15–20 seconds, or until finely chopped. With the motor running, add the oil and continue whizzing until the mixture forms a rough paste. Transfer to a bowl, add the prawns and toss to coat. Set aside to marinate for 30 minutes.

Heat the oil in a large heavy-based saucepan over medium–low heat. Add the bacon, onion, celery and garlic and cook, stirring, for 2 minutes. Reduce the heat, cover and simmer, stirring occasionally, for 5 minutes. Do not allow the bacon and vegetables to brown.

Drain the anchovies on paper towels and pat dry. Roughly chop and add to the bacon mixture. Add the carrot and potato and stir to combine. Cook for 2 minutes, then add the stock and milk. Bring to the boil, then cover and cook for 15 minutes, or until the vegetables are tender.

Remove the saucepan from the heat. Using an immersion blender fitted with the chopping blade, whizz the soup for 20–30 seconds, or until smooth. Add the cream and most of the parsley, reserving some for garnishing. Season well with freshly ground black pepper and keep warm.

Heat a large frying pan over high heat and add the prawns and marinade all at once. Cook, turning, for 2 minutes, or until the prawns are just cooked through.

Place a pile of prawns in the centre of four large soup bowls and ladle the soup around the prawns. Sprinkle with the remaining parsley and serve immediately.

tip The soup will keep in the refrigerator, covered, for up to 2 days. It is not suitable for freezing.

Whizz the garlic, chilli and parsley until the mixture is **finely chopped**.

Drain the **anchovies** on paper towels.

sweet potato, chilli and coriander soup

serves 4

6 whole **coriander (cilantro) plants** (roots, stems and leaves)

1 small **red chilli**, seeded and roughly chopped

2 **garlic cloves**, chopped

1 tablespoon **oil**

1 large **onion**, chopped

1 **celery stalk**, chopped

650 g (1 lb 7 oz) **orange sweet potato**, cut into 5 cm (2 inch) pieces

1 litre (35 fl oz/4 cups) **chicken stock** or **vegetable stock**

145 ml (4³/4 fl oz) **coconut milk**

Remove the leaves from the coriander plants. Reserve a few whole leaves for garnishing and chop the remainder of the leaves. Set aside. Thoroughly wash the roots and stems and chop roughly. Put in a mini processor and add the chilli and garlic. Add 2 teaspoons of the oil and whizz for 20 seconds, or until the mixture forms a rough paste.

Heat the remaining oil in a large heavy-based saucepan. Add the paste and stir over low heat for 2 minutes, or until aromatic. Stir in the onion and celery. Cover and cook for 5 minutes, stirring once or twice. Do not allow the mixture to brown.

Add the sweet potato and stir to coat in the mixture. Cook for 2 minutes, then add the stock. Bring to the boil, then reduce the heat, cover and cook for 20 minutes, or until the sweet potato is tender. Set aside to cool slightly.

Using an immersion blender fitted with the chopping blade, whizz the soup until smooth. Season well with salt and freshly ground black pepper. Stir in the coconut milk and gently reheat the soup. Add the chopped coriander leaves and serve garnished with the reserved whole coriander leaves.

tips The soup can also be served chilled. It will keep in the refrigerator, covered, for up to 5 days, or in an airtight container in the freezer for up to 1 month.

broad bean soup with a mixed herb paste

serves 4

1 kg (2 lb 4 oz) **broad (fava) beans**, shelled

2 tablespoons **olive oil**

2 large **leeks**, white part only, sliced

1 large **onion**, chopped

2 **celery stalks**, sliced

3 **garlic cloves**, finely chopped

50 g (1 3/4 oz) sliced **pancetta**, cut into matchsticks

1 teaspoon **ground cumin**

1.25 litres (44 fl oz/5 cups) **chicken stock** or **vegetable stock**

snipped **chives**, to serve

herb paste

1 small handful **mint**

1 small handful **basil**

1 small handful **flat-leaf (Italian) parsley**

1/2 teaspoon grated **lemon zest**

1 **garlic clove**, chopped

2 tablespoons **toasted pine nuts**

80 ml (2 1/2 fl oz/1/3 cup) **olive oil**

Slip the soaked broad beans out of their **skins**.

Using an immersion blender, **whizz the soup** until it is smooth.

Soak the broad beans in boiling water for 3–4 minutes, then drain. When cool enough to handle, slip off the skins.

Gently heat the oil in a heavy-based frying pan over medium heat. Add the leek, onion and celery and sauté for 6 minutes, or until the vegetables are softened but not browned. Increase the heat to medium–high, add the garlic, pancetta and cumin and fry, stirring constantly, for 1 minute.

Transfer the pancetta mixture to a large saucepan and add the broad beans and stock. Bring to the boil over medium heat, then reduce the heat and simmer for 10 minutes.

Remove the saucepan from the heat. Using an immersion blender fitted with the chopping blade, whizz the soup for 1 minute, or until smooth. Season with salt and freshly ground black pepper, to taste.

To make the herb paste, put the mint, basil, parsley, lemon zest, garlic and pine nuts in a small processor fitted with the metal blade. Whizz until roughly chopped. With the motor running, gradually add the olive oil and continue whizzing for 45–60 seconds, or until the mixture has a paste-like consistency.

Divide the soup among four bowls and top with the herb paste and chives.

jerusalem artichoke soup

serves 4

50 g (1¾ oz) **butter**

1 **onion**, roughly chopped

1 **leek**, white part only, chopped

1 **celery stalk**, chopped

2 **garlic cloves**, chopped

800 g (1 lb 12 oz) **jerusalem artichokes**, cut into 5 cm (2 inch) pieces

2 **potatoes**, about 250 g (9 oz), cut into 5 cm (2 inch) pieces

1 teaspoon freshly grated **nutmeg**

500 ml (17 fl oz/2 cups) **chicken stock** or **vegetable stock**

500 ml (17 fl oz/2 cups) **milk**

2 tablespoons finely snipped **chives**

Heat the butter in a large heavy-based saucepan over low heat. Add the onion, leek, celery and garlic and cook for 2 minutes. Cover and simmer, stirring occasionally, for 5 minutes. Do not allow the vegetables to brown.

Add the jerusalem artichokes, potato and nutmeg and stir to combine. Cook for 2 minutes, then add the stock and 250 ml (9 fl oz/1 cup) of the milk. Bring to the boil, cover and cook for 20 minutes, or until the vegetables are tender.

Remove the saucepan from the heat. Using an immersion blender fitted with the chopping blade, whizz the soup for 10 seconds, or until roughly puréed. Season well with salt and freshly ground black pepper. Stir in the remaining milk and half the chives and gently reheat the soup.

Ladle the soup into four bowls and sprinkle with the remaining chives and some freshly ground black pepper.

tips The jerusalem artichokes can be replaced with an equal weight of potatoes. The soup will keep in the refrigerator, covered, for up to 4 days, or in an airtight container in the freezer for up to 1 month.

spinach and lentil soup

serves 4

250 g (9 oz/1 1/3 cups) **green lentils,** rinsed and picked over

1.5 litres (52 fl oz/6 cups) **chicken stock**

60 ml (2 fl oz/1/4 cup) **olive oil**

1 large **onion,** finely chopped

1 **fennel bulb,** trimmed and finely diced

1 large **carrot,** finely diced

1/2 teaspoon **fennel seeds**

1/4 teaspoon **cayenne pepper**

2 **bay leaves**

90 g (3 1/4 oz/1/3 cup) **tomato paste (concentrated purée)**

3 **garlic cloves,** halved lengthways and thinly sliced

3 large handfuls **baby English spinach,** washed

small pinch of **sweet smoked paprika**

extra virgin olive oil, to serve

Put the lentils in a large saucepan and cover with cold water. Bring to the boil over medium–high heat, then reduce the heat and simmer for 10 minutes. Drain and return to the saucepan. Add the stock and 500 ml (17 fl oz/2 cups) of water and bring to the boil. Reduce the heat to medium and simmer for 15 minutes.

Meanwhile, gently heat 2 tablespoons of the oil in a heavy-based frying pan. Add the onion, fennel, carrot, fennel seeds and cayenne pepper. Lightly crush the bay leaves in your hand and add them to the pan. Sauté over low heat for 5 minutes, or until the onion is translucent but not browned. Stir through the tomato paste. Add the onion mixture to the lentils and simmer, partially covered, for 20 minutes, or until the lentils and vegetables are tender.

Gently heat the remaining oil in a frying pan over low heat. Add the garlic and 2 handfuls of the spinach and cook, stirring, for 2–3 minutes, or until the spinach has wilted. Add the paprika. Add the spinach mixture to the soup and simmer for 2 minutes.

Remove the saucepan from the heat and discard the bay leaves. Transfer half the soup to a blender or small processor fitted with the metal blade. Whizz for 30 seconds, or until smooth. Return the puréed soup to the saucepan and add the remaining spinach. Season to taste. Drizzle with extra virgin olive oil and sprinkle with freshly ground black pepper.

split pea and sweet potato soup

serves 4

80 ml (2¹/2 fl oz/¹/3 cup) **olive oil**

1 large **onion**, chopped

2 **garlic cloves**, finely chopped

2 teaspoons finely chopped fresh **ginger**

120 g (4¹/4 oz/¹/2 cup) **yellow split peas**

1 **red chilli**, seeded and sliced

¹/2 teaspoon **sweet smoked paprika**

1 litre (35 fl oz/4 cups) **chicken stock**

500 g (1 lb 2 oz) **orange sweet potato**, cubed

1 tablespoon finely chopped **mint**

Heat 1 tablespoon of the oil in a large saucepan over medium heat. Fry the onion, garlic and ginger for 4–5 minutes, or until soft and golden. Stir in the split peas, chilli and paprika and cook for 1 minute. Add the stock and bring to the boil. Reduce the heat and simmer for 20 minutes.

Add the sweet potato, return to the boil, then reduce the heat and simmer for 15 minutes, or until the sweet potato is tender.

Meanwhile, heat the remaining oil in a small saucepan over low heat. Stir in the mint, then immediately remove the saucepan from the heat. Transfer the mint and oil to a small dish.

Remove the soup from the heat. Using an immersion blender fitted with the chopping blade, whizz for 30 seconds, or until puréed.

Ladle the soup into four bowls and drizzle with a little of the minted oil.

roasted tomato, almond and basil soup

serves 4

60 ml (2 fl oz/1/4 cup) **olive oil**

1 kg (2 lb 4 oz) large, **vine-ripened tomatoes**

1 large **onion**, finely chopped

2 **garlic cloves**, thinly sliced

50 g (13/4 oz/1/3 cup) **blanched almonds**, roughly chopped

2 handfuls **basil**, roughly torn

750 ml (26 fl oz/3 cups) **chicken stock**

Preheat the oven to 180°C (350°F/Gas 4). Grease a baking tray with 1 tablespoon of the oil. Cut the tomatoes in half, scoop out the seeds and arrange, cut side down, on the prepared tray. Roast for 15 minutes, then remove from the oven and set aside until the tomatoes are cool enough to handle. Discard the tomato skin and roughly chop the flesh.

Heat the remaining oil in a large saucepan over medium–low heat. Gently sauté the onion and garlic for 5–6 minutes, or until soft and translucent. Add the chopped tomato, almonds and half the basil. Fry, stirring once or twice, for 5 minutes.

Transfer the mixture to a small processor fitted with the metal blade and whizz for 15–20 seconds, or until thick and smooth.

Return the mixture to the saucepan, stir in the stock and bring to the boil over medium–high heat. Stir in the remaining basil, season with salt and freshly ground black pepper, to taste, and serve immediately.

Cut the **tomatoes** in half and **scoop out** the seeds.

When the roasted tomatoes are cool enough to handle, **discard** the skins.

sauces, dressings and marinades

saucy sensations

Drizzle, dollop, dip and toss ... sauces, dressings and marinades are the crowning glories of the culinary world. A chargrilled lamb cutlet reaches new heights with the addition of a creamy mint and yoghurt sauce, an Asian dipping sauce spices up chicken skewers, while a bowl of pasta becomes a knock-out when dressed with a fresh and nutty pesto. Many of these recipes have multiple uses, and we've included serving suggestions as well as storage and handling tips to make your busy life easier. Who'd go back to making hollandaise sauce the traditional way after using the fast and fail-safe processor method? Only someone with time to burn and a mini processor on their Christmas list.

asian greens with chilli and coconut marinade

serves 4

marinade

15 g (1/2 oz/1/4 cup) **shredded coconut**

2 **garlic cloves**, roughly chopped

2 cm (3/4 inch) piece **ginger**, roughly chopped

1 **red Asian shallot**, roughly chopped

1 small **red chilli**, sliced

2 tablespoons **oil**

1 tablespoon **rice vinegar**

2 teaspoons **fish sauce**

1 teaspoon **soft brown sugar**

2 **spring onions (scallions)**, sliced

1.1 kg (2 lb 7 oz/2 bunches) **Asian green vegetables**

vegetable oil, for cooking

sesame oil, optional, to serve

To make the marinade, heat a dry frying pan over medium heat. Add the shredded coconut and fry, stirring, for 3–4 minutes, or until brown. Transfer the coconut to a spice mill or mini processor, add the garlic, ginger, shallot and chilli and whizz until finely chopped. Add the oil, vinegar, fish sauce and sugar and whizz in short bursts until blended. Transfer to a large bowl and stir in the spring onion.

Slice the Asian green vegetables into 8 cm (31/4 inch) lengths and divide these into stems and leaves. Heat a wok or large frying pan over medium–high heat and add 2 tablespoons of vegetable oil. Add the vegetable stems and stir-fry for 1 minute. Add the vegetable leaves and stir-fry for 45–60 seconds, or until they wilt and turn bright green.

Transfer the hot vegetables to the bowl with the marinade and toss to coat. Marinate for at least 1 hour to allow the flavours to develop.

Serve the vegetables cold or reheat them in the wok. Drizzle with a little sesame oil, if using.

lamb cutlets with green chilli, mint and yoghurt sauce

serves 4

sauce

1 large **green chilli**, seeded and chopped

1 large handful **mint**

1 **red Asian shallot**, chopped

3 cm (1 1/4 inch) piece **ginger**, chopped

2 teaspoons **fish sauce**

2 teaspoons **lime juice**

1 teaspoon shaved **palm sugar** or **soft brown sugar**

250 g (9 oz/1 cup) **Greek-style yoghurt**

12–16 **French-trimmed lamb cutlets** (see tips)

To make the sauce, put the chilli, mint, shallot, ginger, fish sauce, lime juice and sugar in a small processor fitted with the metal blade. Whizz for 30 seconds, or until the mixture forms a rough paste. Transfer to a small bowl and stir in the yoghurt. Cover and refrigerate until needed.

Brush a chargrill pan with oil, heat over high heat and add the cutlets in a single layer. Cook for 2 minutes on each side, or until the cutlets are browned on the outside but still feel springy when pressed. Season well with salt and freshly ground black pepper.

Arrange the cutlets on a serving plate and serve with the sauce.

tips French-trimmed lamb cutlets have the bones trimmed of fat and sinew. Ask your butcher to prepare the cutlets for you. Couscous or potato mash are ideal accompaniments to this dish. Store the sauce, covered, in the refrigerator for up to 2 days.

hollandaise sauce

makes 185 ml (6 fl oz/3/4 cup)

125 g (4¹/2 oz) **butter**

3 **egg yolks**

1 tablespoon **tarragon vinegar** or **lemon juice**

white pepper, to taste

Tabasco sauce, optional, to taste

Melt the butter in a small saucepan over low heat. Set aside to cool for 10 minutes.

Put the egg yolks in the bowl of a mini processor. Add the vinegar or lemon juice and whizz for 5 seconds, or until combined. With the motor running, gradually add the melted butter, slowly at first, then at a faster rate as the mixture thickens.

Season, to taste, with salt, white pepper and Tabasco, if using. The sauce is best served immediately, but it can be stored if the surface is covered with plastic wrap to prevent a skin from forming.

tip Hollandaise sauce is delicious served over steamed asparagus.

blini with roast capsicum aïoli and beef slivers

serves 4

blini

60 g (2¹/4 oz/¹/2 cup) **self-raising flour**

125 ml (4 fl oz/¹/2 cup) **milk**

1 **egg yolk**

1 teaspoon grated **lemon zest**

aïoli

1 **red capsicum (pepper)**

2 small **garlic cloves**, chopped

2 **egg yolks**

125 ml (4 fl oz/¹/2 cup) **grapeseed oil**

1–2 teaspoons **lemon juice**, to taste

canola oil spray

4 very thin slices (80 g/2³/4 oz) **rare roast beef**

small **lemon thyme sprigs**, to serve

Peel the **blackened** and blistered skin from the **red capsicum**.

Cook the blini until **bubbles appear** on the surface, then turn and **cook** the other side.

To make the blini, put the flour in a small processor fitted with the plastic blade. Add the milk, egg yolk and lemon zest. Whizz in short bursts for 20 seconds, or until smooth. Pour the mixture into a bowl or pitcher and set aside.

To make the aïoli, preheat the grill (broiler) to high. Put the capsicum, skin side up, on the grill rack and grill (broil), turning often, for 12–15 minutes, or until well blackened. Cool in a plastic bag, then peel and discard the skin. Halve, discard the seeds and roughly chop the flesh.

Put the capsicum and garlic in a mini processor. Whizz for 10 seconds, or until smooth. Add the egg yolks and whizz in short bursts until combined. With the motor running, slowly add the oil and process until thick and creamy. Add the lemon juice, to taste, and season well with salt and freshly ground black pepper.

Lightly spray a non-stick frying pan with oil and heat over medium heat. Drop several heaped teaspoons of the blini mixture into the pan to make 5 cm (2 inch) rounds. Cook for 1 minute, or until bubbles appear on the surface, then turn and cook the other side. Transfer to a wire rack and cover with a clean tea towel (dish towel) while you cook the remaining mixture.

Spoon the aïoli onto the blini. Slice each piece of beef into quarters and add a piece to each blini. Serve topped with lemon thyme sprigs.

tips Try salami, pastrami or smoked salmon instead of the beef. Leftover aïoli can be stored in an airtight container in the refrigerator for up to 4 days. Serve it on steamed or boiled vegetables, or barbecued seafood.

penne with zucchini, ricotta and parmesan sauce

serves 4

500 g (1 lb 2 oz/5¹/2 cups) small **penne pasta**

sauce

2 **zucchini (courgettes)**, chopped

2 **garlic cloves**, chopped

1 small **red chilli**, seeded and chopped

125 g (4¹/2 oz/¹/2 cup) **ricotta cheese**

100 ml (3¹/2 fl oz) **pouring cream**

2 teaspoons finely grated **lemon zest**

100 g (3¹/2 oz/1 cup) grated **parmesan cheese**

1 handful **basil**, chopped

small **basil leaves**, to serve

parmesan cheese shavings, to serve

Cook the penne pasta in a large saucepan of boiling salted water according to the manufacturer's instructions. Drain the penne, reserving 125 ml (4 fl oz/¹/2 cup) of the cooking water.

Meanwhile, to make the sauce, put the zucchini, garlic and chilli in a small processor fitted with the metal blade and whizz in short bursts for 30 seconds, or until finely chopped. Add the ricotta, cream, lemon zest, parmesan and chopped basil, and season well with salt and freshly ground black pepper. Whizz for 20 seconds, or until smooth.

Pour the sauce over the hot penne, adding enough of the reserved cooking water to make a coating consistency. Serve immediately, topped with small basil leaves and parmesan shavings.

tip Prepare the sauce just prior to serving. It is not suitable for freezing.

baked sticky pork ribs

serves 4

1 small **navel orange**

1 large **garlic clove**

1/2 **onion**, chopped

1 teaspoon grated fresh **ginger**

90 g (31/4 oz/1/4 cup) **golden syrup** or **dark corn syrup**

1 teaspoon **worcestershire sauce**

4 drops **Tabasco sauce**

2 tablespoons **tomato paste (concentrated purée)**

16 **pork spareribs**

2 **spring onions (scallions)**, green part only, shredded

Put the orange in a small saucepan, cover with water and bring to the boil. Simmer for 3–5 minutes, or until soft. Alternatively, put the orange in a plastic bag and microwave on High (100%) for 3 minutes, or until soft. Set aside to cool.

Cut the orange into large chunks, reserving the juice. Put the orange and juice in a small processor fitted with the metal blade. Add the garlic, onion and ginger and whizz for 25–30 seconds, or until finely chopped. Add the golden syrup or corn syrup, worcestershire sauce, Tabasco sauce and tomato paste and whizz until smooth. Transfer to a shallow dish, add the pork spareribs and rub them with the marinade. Cover and refrigerate for 4 hours.

Preheat the oven to 180°C (350°F/Gas 4). Put the spareribs, side by side, on a large baking tray and roast for 20 minutes. Turn to coat with the sauce, then roast for a further 25–30 minutes, or until tender. Serve hot or at room temperature, topped with spring onions.

open lasagne with rocket and walnut pesto

serves 4

pesto

100 g (3¹/2 oz/1 cup) **walnuts**

2 **garlic cloves**

2 large handfuls **baby rocket (arugula)**

1 large handful **basil**

1 large handful **flat-leaf (Italian) parsley**

100 ml (3¹/2 fl oz) **extra virgin olive oil**

80 ml (2¹/2 fl oz/¹/3 cup) **walnut oil**

50 g (1³/4 oz/¹/2 cup) grated **pecorino cheese**

100 g (3¹/2 oz/1 cup) grated **parmesan cheese**

375 g (13 oz) fresh **lasagne sheets**

1 tablespoon **olive oil**

4 large handfuls **baby English spinach**

1 **garlic clove**, sliced

2 tablespoons **lemon juice**

200 g (7 oz) **marinated goat's feta cheese**, crumbled

2 tablespoons grated **parmesan cheese**

Whizz the **walnuts**, garlic, rocket, basil and parsley until the **mixture** resembles coarse breadcrumbs.

With the motor running, gradually **add the oils** in a thin stream.

To make the pesto, preheat the oven to 180°C (350°F/Gas 4). Rinse the walnuts in cold water, then shake dry. Spread the walnuts on a baking tray and bake for 5–8 minutes, or until lightly golden. Watch carefully as they will burn easily.

Transfer the walnuts to a small processor fitted with the metal blade. Add the garlic, rocket, basil and parsley and whizz in 3-second bursts for 1 minute, or until the mixture resembles coarse breadcrumbs. With the motor running, add the oils in a thin stream, then add the pecorino and parmesan and whizz for 40 seconds. Cover with plastic wrap and set aside.

Cut the lasagne sheets into sixteen 8 cm (3¼ inch) squares. Cook a few squares at a time in a large saucepan of boiling salted water for 4 minutes, or until al dente. Lay them on a clean tea towel (dish towel) and cover to keep warm while the remaining squares are cooked.

Heat the olive oil in a large frying pan over medium heat, add the spinach and garlic and sauté until just wilted. Add the lemon juice and stir to combine. Cover and keep warm.

Spoon 1 tablespoon of the pesto onto four warmed plates and spread out with the back of the spoon to the size of one of the pasta squares. Cover with a pasta square, then divide one-third of the spinach over the pasta. Sprinkle with one-third of the goat's feta, cover with another pasta square and spread with the pesto. Repeat the layers, finishing with a layer of pesto. Sprinkle with the grated parmesan and serve immediately.

tips The pesto is also delicious spooned over steamed vegetables such as green beans and potatoes to accompany grilled (broiled) fish or meat. Store the pesto, covered with a thin layer of olive oil in an airtight container, in the refrigerator for up to 3 days.

thai nam prik sauce

makes 250 ml (9 fl oz/1 cup)

40 g (1 1/2 oz/1/3 cup) **dried shrimp**

1 cm (1/2 inch) cube **shrimp paste**

4 small **red chillies**, seeded and roughly chopped

3 **garlic cloves**, roughly chopped

4 **coriander (cilantro) roots and lower stems**, chopped

1 handful **coriander (cilantro) leaves**, roughly chopped

8 **pea eggplants (aubergines)**

1 tablespoon **fish sauce**

60 ml (2 fl oz/1/4 cup) **lime juice**

1–2 tablespoons shaved **palm sugar** or **soft brown sugar**

Put the dried shrimp in a small heatproof bowl and cover with boiling water. Set aside for 15 minutes, then drain.

Meanwhile, wrap the shrimp paste in foil and fry in a small dry frying pan over medium heat for 5 minutes, turning once or twice.

Put the dried shrimp, shrimp paste, chilli and garlic in a mini processor and whizz in 3-second bursts for 25 seconds, or until roughly chopped. Add the coriander and eggplants and whizz in short bursts until the mixture has a medium–coarse texture. Add the fish sauce, lime juice and sugar and whizz in short bursts until combined. Add 1 teaspoon of water at a time until the sauce reaches a dipping consistency.

tips Use the sauce as a flavouring to stir through steamed rice or meat dishes. Store the sauce in an airtight container in the refrigerator for up to 2 weeks.

cheese tortellini with pistachio and lime sauce

serves 4

3 slices **white bread**, crusts removed

100 g (31/2 oz/2/3 cup) **pistachio kernels**

grated **zest** of 1 **lime**

1 **garlic clove**, chopped

50 g (13/4 oz/1/2 cup) grated **parmesan cheese**

1 handful **flat-leaf (Italian) parsley**

2 teaspoons **thyme**

80 ml (21/2 fl oz/1/3 cup) **olive oil**

500 g (1 lb 2 oz) **cheese tortellini**

grated **parmesan cheese**, to serve

Put the bread in a mini processor and whizz for 30 seconds, or until breadcrumbs form. Remove half of the crumbs and set aside.

Add the pistachios, lime zest, garlic, parmesan, parsley and thyme to the processor containing the remaining crumbs and whizz for 30 seconds, or until the mixture forms a coarse paste. With the motor running, gradually add 60 ml (2 fl oz/1/4 cup) of the oil. Season well with salt and freshly ground black pepper.

Cook the cheese tortellini in a large saucepan of boiling salted water according to the manufacturer's instructions. Drain the tortellini, reserving 250 ml (9 fl oz/1 cup) of the cooking water.

Meanwhile, heat the remaining oil in a small frying pan over medium heat. Add the reserved breadcrumbs and stir for 1–2 minutes, or until lightly golden.

Stir the sauce through the hot tortellini, adding enough of the reserved cooking water to make a coating consistency. Serve immediately, topped with the toasted breadcrumbs and grated parmesan.

fresh tomato sauce

makes 500 ml (17 fl oz/2 cups)

450 g (1 lb) **roma (plum) tomatoes**

pinch of **soft brown sugar**

1 **garlic clove**, finely minced

1/2 teaspoon finely grated **lemon zest**

1 1/2 tablespoons **lemon juice**

few drops of **Tabasco sauce**, or to taste

60 ml (2 fl oz/1/4 cup) **olive oil**

1 teaspoon finely chopped **mint**

Remove the cores from the tomatoes. Roughly chop the flesh and put it in a blender or small processor fitted with the metal blade. Whizz for 1 minute.

Drain the tomato through a fine sieve, discarding the juice. Return the pulp to the blender or processor and add the sugar, garlic, lemon zest and lemon juice. Whizz until just combined. Add salt and Tabasco sauce, to taste. With the motor running, gradually add the oil. Stir the mint through the sauce.

tips Serve the sauce with steamed vegetables, filled pasta or plain fish.
Store the sauce in an airtight container in the refrigerator for up to 5 days.

chargrilled prawn salad with saffron aïoli

serves 4

aïoli
3 teaspoons **lemon juice**

small pinch of **saffron threads**

2 **egg yolks**

3 **garlic cloves**, minced

1 teaspoon **dijon mustard**

230 ml (73/4 fl oz) **olive oil**

1/4–1/2 teaspoon **cayenne pepper**, to taste

250 g (9 oz/11/2 cups) shelled **broad (fava) beans**

16 **asparagus spears**, sliced in half on the diagonal

300 g (101/2 oz) **watercress**

1 **avocado**

250 g (9 oz/2 cups) **yellow teardrop tomatoes**, halved

20 **raw prawns (shrimp)**, peeled and deveined

1 tablespoon **olive oil**

1 teaspoon **lemon juice**

sea salt, to taste

To make the aïoli, put the lemon juice and saffron in a small bowl and set aside for 30 minutes. Transfer to a mini processor and add the egg yolks, garlic and mustard. Whizz for 8–10 seconds, or until smooth, scraping down the side of the bowl if necessary. With the motor running, gradually add the olive oil. Season with salt and cayenne pepper, to taste.

Bring a saucepan of water to the boil and add the broad beans and a large pinch of salt. Simmer over medium heat for 4 minutes. Scoop out the beans with a slotted spoon and rinse under cold water. Add the asparagus to the water and blanch for 1 minute, or until just tender. Drain, rinse under cold water and transfer to a shallow salad bowl.

Peel off and discard the broad bean skins. Add the broad beans to the asparagus. Pick the top leaves from the watercress, leaving some of their stalks on. Halve the avocado, cut the flesh into chunks and add to the salad, along with the watercress and tomatoes.

Preheat the barbecue plate or chargrill pan to medium–high. Toss the prawns in the combined oil and lemon juice and grill for 45 seconds on each side, or until just cooked through.

Add the prawns to the salad, season with sea salt and freshly ground black pepper and toss lightly. Serve the salad accompanied by the aïoli.

Combine the lemon juice and
saffron threads
and soak for 30 minutes.

Add the **broad beans**
and salt to a pan of boiling
water, **then simmer**
for 4 minutes.

potato gnocchi with gorgonzola, goat's cheese and thyme sauce

serves 4

30 g (1 oz/1/4 cup) **roasted skinned hazelnuts**

150 g (51/2 oz) **gorgonzola cheese** or other **strong dry blue cheese**

100 g (31/2 oz) **goat's cheese**

4 tablespoons **thyme**

grated **zest** of 1 **lemon**

750 g (1 lb 10 oz) **potato gnocchi**

80 ml (21/2 fl oz/1/3 cup) **extra virgin olive oil**

2 **leeks**, white part only, thinly sliced

60 ml (2 fl oz/1/4 cup) **pouring cream**

Put the hazelnuts in a mini processor and whizz in 2-second bursts for 20 seconds, or until roughly chopped. Transfer to a small bowl.

Put the gorgonzola or blue cheese, goat's cheese, thyme and lemon zest in the mini processor and whizz in short bursts for 15 seconds, or until crumbled.

Cook the potato gnocchi in a large saucepan of boiling salted water according to the manufacturer's instructions. Drain the gnocchi, return to the pan and toss with a little of the oil.

Meanwhile, heat 2 tablespoons of the oil in a large frying pan over medium–high heat, add the leek and sauté for 5–6 minutes, or until softened. Add the cream and the cheese mixture and cook, stirring, over low heat for 3–5 minutes, or until the cheese has melted.

Add the cheese sauce and remaining oil to the gnocchi and gently toss through. Season with salt and freshly ground black pepper, to taste. Spoon into four bowls, sprinkle with the chopped hazelnuts and serve immediately.

roast tomato and shallot sauce

makes 500 ml (17 fl oz/2 cups)

250 g (9 oz/2 cups) **cherry tomatoes**, halved

3 **French shallots**, quartered

1 tablespoon **extra virgin olive oil**

1/4 teaspoon **caster (superfine) sugar**

30 g (1 oz/1/4 cup) **walnuts**

200 g (7 oz/3/4 cup) **ricotta cheese**

2 teaspoons grated **lemon zest**

2 **garlic cloves**, finely chopped

2 tablespoons **pouring cream**

1 tablespoon finely chopped **dill**

1 tablespoon **salted baby capers**, rinsed and squeezed dry

Preheat the oven to 200°C (400°F/Gas 6). Put the tomatoes and shallots on a baking tray and season with salt and freshly ground black pepper. Toss with the olive oil and sugar. Roast for 20 minutes, or until soft.

Meanwhile, put the walnuts in a small processor fitted with the metal blade and whizz for 12–15 seconds, or until the mixture has a medium–fine consistency. Add the ricotta, lemon zest, garlic and cream and whizz until smooth.

Transfer the walnut mixture to a bowl and add the roasted tomatoes and shallots, dill and capers. Toss lightly, season, to taste, and serve immediately.

tip This sauce is an excellent accompaniment for fried or grilled (broiled) white fish, or it can be served as a pasta sauce. Serve while the fish or pasta is still hot so that the sauce will heat a little more.

chicken skewers with spicy chilli dipping sauce

serves 4

sauce

2 **lemon grass stems**, white part only, chopped

8 **coriander (cilantro) roots** including 10 cm (4 inches) stems, chopped

7 cm (2¾ inch) piece **galangal**, chopped

1 large **red Asian shallot**, chopped

2 **garlic cloves**, chopped

1 large **green chilli**, seeded and chopped

3 large **tomatoes**

1 tablespoon **oil**

60 ml (2 fl oz/¼ cup) **fish sauce**

25 g (1 oz/¼ cup) shaved **palm sugar** or **soft brown sugar**

2 teaspoons **tamarind concentrate**

2 tablespoons chopped **coriander (cilantro) leaves**

750 g (1 lb 10 oz) boneless, skinless **chicken breast**, cubed

canola oil spray or **olive oil spray**

To make the sauce, put the lemon grass, coriander roots and stems, galangal, shallot, garlic and chilli in a small processor fitted with the metal blade. Whizz in 3–4 second bursts for 30 seconds, or until finely chopped.

Score a cross in the base of each tomato. Put in a heatproof bowl and cover with boiling water. Leave for 30 seconds, then transfer to cold water and peel the skin away from the cross. Roughly chop the tomatoes.

Heat the oil in a large heavy-based saucepan. Add the lemon grass paste, stir, then add two-thirds of the chopped tomato. Cook, stirring, for 5 minutes. Set aside to cool slightly, then transfer to the processor and whizz for 15 seconds, or until smooth. Add the remaining tomato and whizz in short bursts for 15 seconds, or until the mixture is finely chopped but still has texture.

Return the mixture to the saucepan and add the fish sauce, sugar and tamarind concentrate. Simmer, stirring frequently, for 10 minutes. Stir in the coriander leaves.

Thread the chicken onto metal skewers and spray with oil. Preheat the barbecue or chargrill pan to high and cook the chicken, turning frequently, for 5–7 minutes, or until just cooked through. Serve immediately, accompanied by the sauce.

Score a cross in the base of each of the tomatoes to assist in **peeling** them.

Heat the oil in a heavy-based **saucepan** and add the lemon grass paste.

barbecue sauce

makes 375 ml (13 fl oz/1 1/2 cups)

1 1/2 tablespoons **oil**

1 large **onion**, chopped

2 **garlic cloves**, minced

2 teaspoons **red wine vinegar**

1 tablespoon **honey**

1 1/2 tablespoons **worcestershire sauce**

1 teaspoon **mustard powder**

400 g (14 oz) tin **chopped tomatoes**

Heat the oil in a large frying pan over low heat. Add the onion and garlic and fry for 6–8 minutes, or until soft. Add the vinegar, honey, worcestershire sauce and mustard powder and fry for 1 minute.

Add the tomatoes and simmer, stirring occasionally, for 20 minutes. Remove from the heat and set aside to cool for 15 minutes.

Transfer the tomato mixture to a blender or small processor fitted with the metal blade and whizz for 20–25 seconds, or until smooth. Season with salt and freshly ground black pepper, to taste.

tips Use the sauce to rub on beef ribs or whole chickens before roasting, or serve with barbecued steaks or sausages. Store the sauce, covered, in the refrigerator for up to 10 days.

sweet chilli sauce

makes 250 ml (9 fl oz/1 cup)

4 long **red chillies**

150 ml (5 fl oz) **rice vinegar**

2 **garlic cloves**, finely chopped

1 tablespoon **fish sauce**, or to taste

125 g (4 oz/1/2 cup) **caster (superfine) sugar**

1 tablespoon shaved **dark palm sugar** or **soft brown sugar** (see tips)

Halve and thinly slice the chillies, discarding the stalks and seeds (or leave the seeds in for a hotter sauce). Put the chilli, vinegar and garlic in a mini processor and whizz for 20–30 seconds, or until very finely chopped. Add the fish sauce and whizz to combine. Add more fish sauce, to taste, if desired.

Put the sugars in a saucepan with 150 ml (5 fl oz) of water. Cook, stirring, over medium–low heat until the sugars have dissolved. Bring to the boil, then reduce the heat and simmer for 1 minute.

Add the chilli mixture to the saucepan and simmer over low heat for 15 minutes, or until slightly thickened. Set aside to cool before serving.

tips Use the sauce as a dipping sauce for spring rolls and fish cakes, as a marinade for chicken, or add it to a stir-fry. Store the sauce in a clean jar in the refrigerator for 3–4 weeks. Shake before using. Dark palm sugar is sold in logs at Asian supermarkets. It is a rich brown colour and is softer than ordinary palm sugar.

thai fish cakes with ginger and lime dipping sauce

serves 4–6

fish cakes

500 g (1 lb 2 oz) skinless **white fish fillets**, roughly chopped

30 g (1 oz/1/4 cup) **cornflour (cornstarch)**

2 tablespoons **red curry paste**

2 tablespoons **fish sauce**

1 **egg**, lightly beaten

3 **spring onions (scallions)**, finely chopped

50 g (13/4 oz) **green beans**, thinly sliced

vegetable oil, for deep-frying

dipping sauce

1 large **red chilli**, seeded and chopped

2 **garlic cloves**, chopped

3 cm (11/4 inch) piece **ginger**, chopped

1/4 small **red onion**, chopped

125 ml (4 fl oz/1/2 cup) **lime juice**

60 ml (2 fl oz/1/4 cup) **fish sauce**

1 tablespoon shaved **palm sugar** or **soft brown sugar**

2 teaspoons **light soy sauce**

To make the fish cakes, put the fish in a processor fitted with the metal blade and whizz for 10 seconds. Add the cornflour, curry paste, fish sauce and egg. Whizz for 20 seconds, or until thoroughly combined. Transfer to a bowl and stir in the spring onion and beans. Using wet hands, form the mixture into twenty-four 4 cm (11/2 inch) flat cakes. Refrigerate, uncovered, for at least 30 minutes to allow the fish cakes to dry out a little.

Meanwhile, to make the dipping sauce, put the chilli, garlic, ginger and red onion in a mini processor and whizz in short bursts for 15 seconds, or until thoroughly chopped. Add the lime juice, fish sauce, sugar and soy sauce. Whizz in short bursts until combined.

Fill a deep-fryer or large heavy-based saucepan one-third full of oil and heat to 180°C (350°F), or until a cube of bread dropped into the oil turns golden brown in 15 seconds. Fry the fish cakes in batches for 3–4 minutes, or until well browned and cooked through. Drain on paper towels. Serve the fish cakes accompanied by the dipping sauce.

steamed pork dumplings with chilli dipping sauce

serves 4

dipping sauce

2 **garlic cloves**, finely minced

125 ml (4 fl oz/1/2 cup) **lime juice**

60 ml (2 fl oz/1/4 cup) **fish sauce**

2 tablespoons **soy sauce**

1 teaspoon **sesame oil**

3 **red chillies**, seeded and finely sliced

1 teaspoon **sesame oil**

2 **red Asian shallots**, finely chopped

1 **garlic clove**, finely chopped

50 g (13/4 oz) **shiitake mushrooms**, roughly chopped

200 g (7 oz) **pork loin**, cubed

1 **Chinese sausage**, finely diced (see tip, page 181)

1 tablespoon finely chopped fresh **ginger**

grated **zest** of 1/2 **orange**

2 teaspoons **soy sauce**

1 small handful **coriander (cilantro) leaves**

24 **won ton wrappers** or **gow gee wrappers**

2 tablespoons **peanut oil**

Put the **pork**, Chinese sausage, ginger, orange zest, soy sauce and **coriander** in a small processor fitted with the **metal blade**.

Gather the edges of the wrapper around the filling and **pinch the edges** to seal the dumpling.

To make the dipping sauce, put the garlic, lime juice, fish sauce, soy sauce and sesame oil in a small bowl and whisk to combine. Pour into a serving dish and sprinkle with the chilli.

Gently heat the sesame oil in a small heavy-based frying pan over low heat. Increase the heat to medium and add the shallots, garlic and mushrooms. Fry, stirring often, for 3–4 minutes, or until the mushrooms have softened. Remove from the heat and set aside.

Put the pork, Chinese sausage, ginger, orange zest, soy sauce and coriander leaves in a small processor fitted with the metal blade and whizz in 3-second bursts for 25 seconds, or until the mixture is finely chopped. Add the mushroom mixture and whizz in short bursts for 12–15 seconds, or until just combined.

Put 2 teaspoons of the pork mixture in the centre of a won ton or gow gee wrapper. Lightly brush the edges with water, then gather the edges together, pinching them to seal. Stand upright and press down lightly to create a flat base. Repeat with the remaining mixture and wrappers.

Heat the peanut oil in a large non-stick frying pan over medium–high heat. Add half the dumplings, making sure they are not touching. Pour 500 ml (17 fl oz/2 cups) of water into the pan, cover tightly and steam for 6–8 minutes. Remove the lid, increase the heat to high and cook, shaking the pan occasionally to prevent the dumplings from sticking and burning, for 4–5 minutes, or until the remaining liquid bubbles and evaporates. The dumplings are ready when the tops are soft and translucent and the bases are crispy and golden. Transfer to a warm platter and keep warm while you cook the remaining dumplings. Serve hot, accompanied by the dipping sauce.

tip Chinese sausages (lap cheong) are slightly sweet, dried pork sausages. They require cooking before use, and are available from Chinese grocers and supermarkets.

lemon rocket pesto

makes 375 ml (13 fl oz/1¹/2 cups)

2 **garlic cloves**, crushed

50 g (1³/4 oz/¹/3 cup) **roasted skinned hazelnuts**

150 g (5¹/2 oz/1 bunch) **rocket (arugula)**, stems removed

50 g (1³/4 oz/¹/2 cup) roughly grated **pecorino pepato cheese**

1 teaspoon grated **lemon zest**

1¹/2 tablespoons **lemon juice**

150 ml (5 fl oz) **olive oil**

Put the garlic and hazelnuts in a small processor fitted with the metal blade and whizz for 10 seconds, or until roughly chopped. Add half the rocket, the pecorino pepato, lemon zest and lemon juice and whizz for 10 seconds.

Scrape down the side of the bowl and add the remaining rocket. Whizz in 2-second bursts until evenly chopped, but not fine. Don't worry if the rocket doesn't break down at this stage. With the motor running, gradually add the olive oil. Whizz until combined but not completely smooth, as a little texture is desirable.

tips The pesto is delicious stirred through pasta or served with poultry, fish or sausages. Store the pesto, covered with a thin layer of olive oil in an airtight container, in the refrigerator for 3–4 days.

blue eye cod with garlic and parsley mayonnaise

serves 4

mayonnaise
3 **garlic cloves**, chopped
2 tablespoons chopped **flat-leaf**
   (Italian) parsley
2 **egg yolks**
1 teaspoon finely grated **lime zest**
1/2 teaspoon **dijon mustard**
125 ml (4 fl oz/1/2 cup) **grapeseed oil**
2–3 teaspoons **lime juice**, to taste

20 g (3/4 oz) **butter**
2 teaspoons **grapeseed oil**
4 skinless **blue eye cod fillets** or other
   large-fleshed white fish fillets

To make the mayonnaise, put the garlic and parsley in a mini processor and whizz in 3-second bursts for 30 seconds, or until finely chopped. Add the egg yolks, lime zest and mustard. With the motor running, gradually add the oil and whizz for 25–40 seconds, or until thick and creamy. Add the lime juice, to taste, and season well with salt and freshly ground black pepper. Whizz briefly to combine.

Heat the butter and oil in a large non stick frying pan over medium heat. Add the fish fillets and cook for 3–4 minutes each side, or until cooked through. Drain on paper towels.

Transfer the fish to warm serving plates and top with some of the mayonnaise.

tips Creamy polenta and a tomato salad are ideal accompaniments to this dish. Store any leftover mayonnaise in an airtight jar in the refrigerator for up to 1 week.

harissa with vegetable couscous

serves 4

harissa

3 **dried bird's eye chillies**

3 large **garlic cloves**

1 teaspoon **coriander seeds**

1/2 teaspoon **ground cumin**

60 ml (2 fl oz/1/4 cup) **extra virgin olive oil**

60 ml (2 fl oz/1/4 cup) **tomato passata (puréed tomatoes)**

1 tablespoon **tomato paste (concentrated purée)**

2 tablespoons roughly chopped **coriander (cilantro)**

2 tablespoons roughly chopped **mint**

250 g (9 oz/1 cup) **Greek-style yoghurt**

300 g (101/2 oz/12/3 cups) **couscous**

60 ml (2 fl oz/1/4 cup) **olive oil**

1 large **onion,** halved and thinly sliced

3 **zucchini (courgettes),** thinly sliced

2 large **carrots,** cut into fine matchsticks 2 cm (3/4 inch) long

400 g (14 oz) tin **chickpeas,** rinsed and drained

40 g (11/2 oz/1/3 cup) **sultanas (golden raisins)**

30 g (1 oz/1/4 cup) **toasted slivered almonds**

2 tablespoons **baby capers,** rinsed and squeezed dry

Whizz the chillies, garlic, coriander seeds and cumin until roughly **ground**.

Combine the chopped coriander, mint and yoghurt.

To make the harissa, put the chillies, garlic, coriander seeds and cumin in a mini processor. Whizz for 30 seconds, or until roughly ground. Add the olive oil, tomato passata and tomato paste and whizz for 12–15 seconds, or until smooth.

Put the coriander, mint and yoghurt in a small bowl and mix to combine.

Prepare the couscous according to the manufacturer's instructions. Cover and set aside. Heat the oil in a large frying pan over medium heat. Add the onion and fry for 5–6 minutes, or until softened. Add the zucchini and carrot and fry for 5 minutes, or until just tender and beginning to brown. Stir in the chickpeas and sultanas. Add the couscous, stirring gently until well combined.

Divide the couscous mixture among four plates and sprinkle with the toasted almonds and capers. Serve accompanied by the harissa and herbed yoghurt, to be added as desired.

tip Store the harissa, covered with a thin layer of olive oil in an airtight container, in the refrigerator for 7–10 days.

spanish tapas dressing

makes 250 ml (9 fl oz/1 cup)

80 ml (2¹/2 fl oz/¹/3 cup) **orange juice**

pinch of **saffron threads**

125 ml (4 fl oz/¹/2 cup) **extra virgin olive oil**

2 tablespoons **lemon juice**

2 **garlic cloves**, finely chopped

1 **bird's eye chilli**, finely chopped

3 tablespoons chopped **dill**

sea salt, to taste

Put the orange juice and saffron in a small saucepan and gently warm over low heat. Remove from the heat and set aside for 5 minutes.

Put the oil, lemon juice, garlic and chilli in a blender or small processor fitted with the metal blade and whizz for 30 seconds, or until well combined. Add the dill and the orange juice and saffron mixture and whizz for 30 seconds. Season with sea salt and freshly ground black pepper, to taste.

tips Use the dressing sparingly over warm vegetables or chargrilled meats and seafood. Store the dressing in an airtight container in the refrigerator for 5–7 days.

cold chicken and mango salad with honey dressing

serves 4

dressing

60 ml (2 fl oz/1/4 cup) **rice vinegar**

2 tablespoons **honey**

3 cm (11/4 inch) piece **ginger**, chopped

60 ml (2 fl oz/1/4 cup) **grapeseed oil**

1 teaspoon **sesame oil**

125 g (41/2 oz) mixed **Asian salad leaves**

1 large **mango**, thinly sliced

125 g (41/2 oz/1 cup) **yellow or red cherry tomatoes**, halved

1/2 small **red onion**, sliced into thin wedges

1 cold **barbecued chicken**, fat and skin removed, meat shredded

30 g (1 oz/3/4 cup) **snow pea (mangetout) sprouts**, trimmed

2 teaspoons **toasted sesame seeds**

To make the dressing, put the vinegar, honey and ginger in a mini processor and whizz in 3-second bursts for 20 seconds, or until finely chopped. With the motor running, slowly pour in the oils and whizz for 20 seconds, or until thick and creamy.

Arrange the salad leaves on individual plates and top with the mango, tomatoes, onion, chicken and snow pea sprouts. Drizzle with the dressing and sprinkle with the sesame seeds. Serve immediately.

beef salad with garlic and red chilli dressing

serves 4

dressing

1–2 **garlic cloves**, chopped

1 **red chilli**, seeded and chopped

3 **coriander (cilantro) roots**, chopped

30 g (1 oz/1/3 cup) shaved **palm sugar** or **soft brown sugar**

2 tablespoons **light soy sauce**

2 tablespoons **lime juice**

1 tablespoon **fish sauce**

600 g (1 lb 5 oz) **thick beef sirloin**, trimmed

olive oil spray

4 **vine-ripened tomatoes**, cut into wedges

1 small **yellow capsicum (pepper)**, seeded and thinly sliced

1/4 small **red onion**, cut into thin wedges

1 large handful **mint**

1 large handful **coriander (cilantro) leaves**

125 g (41/2 oz) mixed **Asian salad leaves**

50 g (13/4 oz/1/3 cup) **roasted peanuts**, roughly chopped

To make the dressing, put the garlic, chilli and coriander roots in a mini processor and whizz for 10 seconds, or until finely chopped. Add the sugar and whizz for 5 seconds. Add the soy sauce, lime juice and fish sauce and whizz for 15 seconds, or until combined.

Preheat the barbecue or chargrill pan to high. Lightly spray the beef with oil and fry for 6 minutes, or until done to your liking. Cover with foil and set aside for 5 minutes.

Slice the beef thinly across the grain. Transfer to a large bowl and add the tomato, capsicum, onion, mint and coriander leaves. Toss to combine. Put the salad leaves on individual plates or a serving platter. Arrange the salad on top of the leaves, sprinkle with the peanuts and drizzle with the dressing. Serve immediately.

seared tuna with mild chilli and orange dressing

serves 4

dressing

zest and juice of 1 orange

1 tablespoon finely chopped rosemary

1 small handful mint

1 very small handful flat-leaf (Italian)
  parsley

1 bird's eye chilli, seeded and finely
  chopped

1 tablespoon red wine vinegar

2 tablespoons walnut oil

80 ml (2¹/₂ fl oz/¹/₃ cup) extra virgin
  olive oil

400 g (14 oz) tin chickpeas, drained

1 small red onion, thinly sliced

1 large handful baby English spinach

4 tuna steaks, 2.5 cm (1 inch) thick

1 tablespoon olive oil

sea salt, to taste

To make the dressing, put the orange zest, rosemary, mint, parsley and chilli in a small processor fitted with the metal blade. Whizz for 30–40 seconds, or until finely chopped. With the motor running, add the orange juice, vinegar and oils and whizz for 20 seconds.

Put the chickpeas, onion and spinach in a bowl, add 2 teaspoons of the dressing and toss to combine.

Brush the tuna steaks with the olive oil and season with sea salt and freshly ground black pepper. Preheat the barbecue plate or chargrill to high. Add the tuna and cook until done to your liking.

Serve the tuna on a bed of chickpea salad, drizzled with the remaining dressing.

walnut and chilli pesto

makes 270 ml (9¹/2 fl oz)

1–2 small **red chillies**, seeded and finely chopped (see tips, page 201)

1 **garlic clove**

50 g (1³/4 oz/¹/2 cup) **walnut pieces**

80 g (2³/4 oz) **parmesan cheese**, cut into thick matchsticks

150 g (5¹/2 oz/1 bunch) **flat-leaf (Italian) parsley**, stalks removed

150 ml (5 fl oz) **olive oil**

Add the **parsley** to the walnut and chilli mixture and **whizz** until combined.

With the motor running, gradually **add the** olive oil to the walnut mixture.

Put the chilli, garlic and walnuts in a small processor fitted with the metal blade and whizz for 10 seconds, or until roughly chopped.

With the motor running, gradually add the parmesan and whizz until the parmesan is evenly chopped.

Scrape down the side of the bowl, add the parsley and whizz for 10 seconds. Scrape the side of the bowl again.

With the motor running, gradually add the olive oil. Whizz until well combined but still with a little texture. You may need to scrape down the side of the bowl a few times while adding the oil. Season with salt, to taste.

tips If you prefer a hotter pesto, leave a few of the chilli seeds in. The pesto is delicious served spread on toasted crusty bread, tossed through pasta or on vegetables as an accompaniment to meat or poultry. Store the pesto, covered with a thin layer of olive oil in an airtight container, in the refrigerator for up to 5 days.

mustard, honey and chive butter

makes a 20 cm (8 inch) log

250 g (9 oz) **butter**, softened

1 tablespoon **honey**

2 **garlic cloves**, roughly chopped

1 1/2 tablespoons snipped **chives**

1 1/2 tablespoons **wholegrain mustard**

1 1/2 teaspoons grated **orange zest**

Put the butter, honey and garlic in a small processor fitted with the plastic blade and whizz for 30 seconds, or until smooth and fluffy. Scrape down the side of the bowl as needed. Add the chives, mustard and orange zest and season with salt and freshly ground black pepper. Whizz just until combined.

Spoon the butter onto a sheet of plastic wrap, moulding it into a rough log shape. Gently guide the wrap around the butter to form a 20 cm (8 inch) cylinder. Twist the ends to tighten and wrap the log in a sheet of foil. Chill until ready to use.

To serve, cut 1 cm (1/2 inch) slices of butter and place on hot steaks or fish to melt, creating a sauce.

tip Store the butter in the refrigerator for up to 1 week. Alternatively, it can be frozen and sliced as needed.

barbecued pork fillet with green peppercorn and mustard sauce

serves 4

sauce

20 g (3/4 oz) **butter**

1 **French shallot**, chopped

1/2 **green capsicum (pepper)**, seeded and chopped

1 **garlic clove**, chopped

90 g (31/4 oz) tin **green peppercorns**, rinsed and drained

1 tablespoon **dijon mustard**

1 tablespoon **lemon juice**

60 ml (2 fl oz/1/4 cup) **pouring cream**

1 teaspoon **soft brown sugar**

2 x 300 g (101/2 oz) **pork fillets**, trimmed

olive oil spray

1 tablespoon chopped **flat-leaf (Italian) parsley**

To make the sauce, heat the butter in a saucepan over low heat. Add the shallot, capsicum and garlic and cook for 5 minutes, or until softened but not browned. Transfer to a mini processor and whizz for 15 seconds, or until puréed. Add the peppercorns, mustard, lemon juice, cream and sugar and whizz for 25–35 seconds, or until the sauce reaches the desired consistency. Return the sauce to the saucepan and keep warm.

Preheat the barbecue plate or chargrill pan. Lightly spray the pork fillets with oil and cook, turning often, for 15–20 minutes, or until just done. Cover with foil and set aside for 5 minutes.

Slice the pork fillets on the diagonal and pile on the centre of four serving plates. Spoon the sauce over the pork and sprinkle with the parsley.

tip Store the sauce, covered, in the refrigerator for up to 3 days.

ocean trout fillets with coriander and lime cream

serves 4

cream

1 large handful **coriander (cilantro) leaves**

2 tablespoons chopped **coriander (cilantro) stems**

grated **zest** of 1 **lime**

1 tablespoon **lime juice**

150 g (5¹/2 oz/²/3 cup) **crème fraîche** or **sour cream**

4 x 185 g (6¹/2 oz) **ocean trout fillets**, skin on

olive oil, for brushing

sea salt, to taste

snow pea sprouts, trimmed, to serve

lime wedges, to serve

To make the cream, put the coriander leaves and stems, lime zest, lime juice and crème fraîche or sour cream in a blender or small processor fitted with the metal blade. Whizz for 35–50 seconds, or until the mixture is creamy.

Preheat the barbecue or chargrill pan to high. Brush both sides of the ocean trout fillets with a little olive oil and rub the skin well with sea salt and freshly ground black pepper. Reduce the heat to medium and add the trout fillets, skin side down. Fry for 3 minutes each side for medium, or until done to your liking. Remove from the heat and rest in a warm place for 2 minutes.

Arrange the trout fillets on a bed of snow pea sprouts on four serving plates, skin side down, and spoon a dollop of coriander and lime cream on top. Serve with lime wedges.

tip The cream can be made in advance and chilled in an airtight container for up to 45 minutes before use. It will change texture if left any longer.

beef in red wine and orange marinade

serves 4

marinade

2 large **onions**, quartered

6 **garlic cloves**

1 tablespoon **thyme**

1 teaspoon **caraway seeds**

zest and **juice** of 1 **orange**

500 ml (17 fl oz/2 cups) **dry red wine**

1 kg (2 lb 4 oz) **chuck steak** or **stewing steak**, cut into 3 cm (1 1/4 inch) cubes

2 tablespoons **olive oil**

6 **bacon slices**, diced

12 **baby onions**

80 g (2 3/4 oz/1/2 cup) pitted **kalamata olives**

200 ml (7 fl oz) **beef stock**

2 **bay leaves**

thyme sprigs, to garnish

To make the marinade, put the onion, garlic, thyme and caraway seeds in a small processor fitted with the metal blade. Whizz for 1 minute, or until the mixture forms a paste. With the motor running, add the orange zest, orange juice and red wine. Whizz for 30 seconds. Transfer to a large bowl.

Add the beef to the marinade, tossing to ensure that all the beef is coated. Cover and refrigerate overnight.

Using tongs, transfer the beef from the marinade to a large bowl and set aside. Strain the marinade.

Heat the oil in a large heavy-based saucepan or flameproof casserole dish, add the diced bacon and fry over medium–high heat for 2 minutes, or until crisp. Remove with a slotted spoon and set aside. Increase the heat to high and brown the beef in small batches.

Return all the beef to the pan and add the reserved marinade, bacon, onions, olives, stock and bay leaves. Bring to the boil, then reduce the heat to low, cover the pan with a sheet of baking paper and put the lid on. Simmer very gently for 1 1/2 hours. Season with salt and freshly ground black pepper, to taste. Garnish with thyme.

tip Steamed rice or potato mash are ideal accompaniments to this dish.

Add the **beef cubes** to the **red wine** and orange marinade.

Fry the diced bacon over medium–high heat for 2 minutes, or **until crisp**.

romesco sauce

makes 375 ml (13 fl oz/1 1/2 cups)

2 large **roma (plum) tomatoes**

60 ml (2 fl oz/1/4 cup) **olive oil**

1/2 small **onion**, finely chopped

2 **garlic cloves,** thinly sliced

1/2 **red capsicum (pepper)**, seeded and diced

1/2 teaspoon **chilli powder**

pinch of **sweet smoked paprika**

1 thick slice **crusty white bread**, lightly toasted

1 1/2 tablespoons **toasted slivered almonds**

1 1/2 tablespoons **red wine vinegar**

Score a cross in the base of the tomatoes. Put in a heatproof bowl and cover with boiling water. Leave for 30 seconds, then transfer to cold water and peel the skin away from the cross. Cut the tomatoes in half, scoop out and discard the seeds and chop the tomato flesh.

Heat 2 tablespoons of the oil in a large heavy-based frying pan over medium heat and sauté the onion and garlic for 3–4 minutes, or until soft and translucent. Add the tomato, capsicum, chilli powder, paprika and 60 ml (2 fl oz/1/4 cup) of water. Cover and simmer gently over low–medium heat for 10 minutes.

Meanwhile, put the bread and almonds in a small processor fitted with the metal blade. Whizz for 20 seconds, or until the mixture resembles coarse breadcrumbs. Add the vinegar and remaining oil and whizz for 10–15 seconds, or until combined.

With the motor running, add the tomato mixture in large spoonfuls and whizz for 20 seconds. Serve warm.

tips This sauce makes a fantastic accompaniment to any grilled (broiled) or steamed seafood but is especially good with chargrilled shellfish, or spooned over steamed mussels. Store the sauce in an airtight container in the refrigerator for up to 7 days.

red pesto

makes 185 ml (6 fl oz/3/4 cup)

4 small **anchovy fillets**

1 tablespoon **dry breadcrumbs**

1 tablespoon **milk**

1/2 large **red capsicum (pepper)**, quartered and seeded

1 **garlic clove**, minced

1 1/2 tablespoons **toasted pine nuts**

1 teaspoon **capers**, rinsed and squeezed dry

1 small handful **basil**, torn

1 1/2 tablespoons **tomato passata (puréed tomatoes)**

1 tablespoon **red wine vinegar**

60 ml (2 fl oz/1/4 cup) **olive oil**

Put the anchovies, breadcrumbs and milk in a small bowl and set aside to soak for 30 minutes.

Preheat the grill (broiler) to high. Arrange the capsicum, skin side up, on a wire rack and grill (broil) for 12–15 minutes, or until the skin blisters. Cool in a plastic bag, then peel and discard the skin. Roughly chop the flesh.

Put the anchovy mixture in a mini processor and add the garlic, pine nuts, capers and basil. Whizz for 30 seconds, or until the mixture forms a coarse paste. Add the capsicum and whizz for 25–35 seconds, or until smooth. Add the tomato passata and vinegar and whizz until just combined. With the motor running, gradually add the oil and whizz until smooth.

tips If serving the pesto on pasta, stir a little of the hot pasta cooking water through the pesto to give a coating consistency. The pesto is also good tossed through hot vegetables. Store the pesto, covered, in the refrigerator for up to 5 days.

chicken satay

serves 4

1 tablespoon **mild curry powder**

1 tablespoon **fish sauce**

1 tablespoon shaved **palm sugar** or **soft brown sugar**

2 **garlic cloves**, roughly chopped

1 tablespoon **chopped coriander (cilantro) stems**

80 ml (2 1/2 fl oz/1/3 cup) **oil**

12 **chicken tenderloins**

1 small handful **coriander (cilantro) leaves**

2–3 tablespoons **fried shallots** (see tips, page 218)

satay sauce

1 tablespoon **tamarind pulp**

125 ml (4 fl oz/1/2 cup) **boiling water**

350 g (12 oz/2 1/4 cups) **roasted peanuts**

500 ml (17 fl oz/2 cups) **coconut cream**

1 tablespoon **red curry paste**

1 tablespoon shaved **palm sugar** or **soft brown sugar**

1 tablespoon **kecap manis** (see tips, page 218)

2 tablespoons **fish sauce**

1 tablespoon **lime juice**

1 **makrut (kaffir lime) leaf**

1/2–2 teaspoons **chilli sauce**, to taste

Combine the curry powder, fish sauce, sugar, garlic, coriander stems and oil in a mini processor and whizz for 40 seconds, or until smooth. Thread each chicken tenderloin onto a bamboo skewer and place in a shallow ceramic or glass dish. Pour the marinade over the skewers, turning to coat the chicken. Cover and chill for 3–4 hours, or overnight.

To make the satay sauce, put the tamarind pulp in a heatproof bowl, add the boiling water and soak for 30 minutes. Mash the pulp with a fork and strain the liquid through a fine sieve. Reserve the liquid and discard the pulp.

Put the peanuts in a small processor fitted with the metal blade and whizz until roughly ground (don't chop the nuts too finely as some texture is desirable). Add the coconut cream, curry paste, sugar, kecap manis, fish sauce, lime juice and 2 tablespoons of tamarind water. Whizz for 1–2 minutes, or until well combined. Transfer to a wok or large saucepan.

Add the lime leaf to the peanut mixture and bring to the boil over medium heat. Stir in the chilli sauce, to taste. Reduce the heat to low and simmer, stirring often, for 10 minutes, being careful not to let it boil or the coconut cream may split.

Preheat the barbecue or chargrill pan to high. Cook the chicken skewers, turning several times, for 5 minutes, or until cooked through.

Arrange the chicken skewers on a platter, sprinkle the coriander and fried shallots on top and spoon over the warm satay sauce.

tips Fried shallots are available from Asian grocery stores and larger supermarkets. Kecap manis is a sweet Indonesian soy sauce. If unavailable, use soy sauce sweetened with a little soft brown sugar.

Pour the **marinade** over the chicken skewers, **turning to coat** the chicken.

Mash the soaked tamarind pulp with **a fork** and discard the pulp.

pork with hoisin, garlic and five-spice marinade

serves 4

marinade

3.5 cm (1 1/2 inch) piece **ginger**, chopped

2 **garlic cloves**, chopped

1/2 **green chilli**, seeded and chopped

1 tablespoon shaved **palm sugar** or **soft brown sugar**

2 tablespoons **hoisin sauce**

1 tablespoon **fish sauce**

1 tablespoon **soy sauce**

1 tablespoon **rice vinegar**

2 teaspoons **sesame oil**

1/2 teaspoon **Chinese five-spice**

2 x 350 g (12 oz) **pork fillets**, trimmed

To make the marinade, put the ginger, garlic, chilli and sugar in a mini processor and whizz for 20 seconds, or until finely chopped. Add the hoisin sauce, fish sauce, soy sauce, vinegar, oil and five-spice and whizz for 10 seconds, or until smooth.

Put the pork fillets in a flat non-metallic dish and pour over the marinade. Cover and refrigerate for at least 2 hours, or overnight. Turn once or twice.

Preheat the barbecue or chargrill pan to medium. Add the pork fillets and cook for 20 minutes, or until done to your liking. Turn frequently and brush with the marinade from time to time. Remove from the heat, cover with foil and set aside for 5 minutes.

Thinly slice the pork fillets on the diagonal. Serve hot or cold.

tips Steamed rice and stir-fried vegetables are ideal accompaniments to this dish. Store the marinade, covered, in the refrigerator for up to 1 week. It can also be used to marinate chicken, pork or beef skewers.

221

chicken with moroccan marinade

serves 4

marinade

2 large **oranges**

2 teaspoons finely chopped fresh
  ginger

2 **garlic cloves**

1 teaspoon **ground turmeric**

1 teaspoon **cardamom seeds**

1/2 teaspoon **cumin seeds**

1/2 teaspoon **paprika**

60 ml (2 fl oz/1/4 cup) **lemon juice**

2 tablespoons **orange marmalade**

1/2 cup (4 fl oz/125 ml) **olive oil**

1 large **chicken**, cut into 8 pieces

12 large **green olives**

40 g (11/2 oz/1/3 cup) **toasted slivered
  almonds**

To make the marinade, zest the oranges, then peel off all the white pith. Remove the segments by cutting between the membranes. Put the orange zest, orange segments, ginger, garlic, turmeric, cardamom seeds, cumin seeds, paprika, lemon juice and marmalade in a small processor fitted with the metal blade. Whizz for 40 seconds, or until combined. With the motor running, pour in the olive oil and whizz for 30 seconds.

Arrange the chicken in an ovenproof dish or roasting tin, spoon over the marinade and rub it into the chicken with your hands. Cover the dish with plastic wrap and set aside for 30 minutes. Preheat the oven to 190°C (375°F/Gas 5).

Remove the plastic wrap from the baking dish. Sprinke the olives around the chicken pieces, cover the dish with foil and bake for 25 minutes. Remove the foil, increase the heat to 220°C (425°F/Gas 7) and bake for 12–15 minutes, or until the chicken is golden. Serve sprinkled with the almonds.

whole fish with garlic and coriander marinade

serves 4

marinade

4 large **garlic cloves**, chopped

4 **coriander (cilantro) roots** including 10 cm (4 inches) stems, chopped

1 teaspoon **white peppercorns**

1 tablespoon **oyster sauce**

1 tablespoon **light soy sauce**

1 teaspoon **fish sauce**

1.25 kg (2 lb 12 oz) **whole snapper**, scaled and cleaned,

   or 2 x 750 g (1 lb 10 oz) snapper

1–2 **banana leaves**

vegetable oil spray

1 small handful chopped **coriander (cilantro) leaves and stems**

To make the marinade, put the garlic, coriander roots and stems and peppercorns in a mini processor and whizz for 10–15 seconds, or until chopped. Add the oyster sauce, soy sauce and fish sauce and whizz for 20 seconds, or until smooth.

Pat the fish dry with paper towels. Slash the flesh on each side two to three times. Layer pieces of banana leaves evenly over a large sheet of foil and lightly spray with oil. Put the fish on the banana leaves.

Spoon the marinade evenly over the fish, including in the cavity. Put the chopped coriander leaves and stems in the cavity. Enclose the fish in the banana leaves and foil and seal. Refrigerate for 2 hours.

Preheat the barbecue to medium. Cook the wrapped fish, turning occasionally, for 25–30 minutes. Open the parcel and check for doneness. If the flesh is not opaque all the way through, return to the heat until cooked.

Carefully unwrap the fish and transfer to a serving platter. Serve immediately.

tip Steamed jasmine rice and lime wedges are ideal accompaniments to this dish.

Pat the fish dry with paper towels and **slash** the flesh two to three times.

Spoon the **marinade** evenly over the fish and **into the cavity**.

marinated sashimi salmon

serves 4

marinade

2 tablespoons crushed **green peppercorns**

3 cm (1 1/4 inch) piece **ginger**, roughly chopped

2 **red Asian shallots**, thinly sliced

1 tablespoon **soy sauce**

125 ml (4 fl oz/1/2 cup) **sake**

125 ml (4 fl oz/1/2 cup) **mirin**

400 g (14 oz) piece **sashimi salmon**, skinned and boned

soy sauce, to serve

pickled ginger, to serve

wasabi, to serve

To make the marinade, put the green peppercorns, ginger, shallots, soy sauce, sake and mirin in a blender or small processor fitted with the metal blade and whizz for 1 minute.

Slice the salmon into 3 mm (1/8 inch) slices and arrange over the base of a large flat-bottomed glass dish. Pour the marinade over the salmon, gently moving the fish around to ensure it is completely covered. Cover and refrigerate for 1 1/2 hours.

Arrange the salmon on a serving platter. Serve with some soy sauce, pickled ginger and wasabi in separate dishes for diners to help themselves.

crusts, pastes and spreads

spread it round

There's something very satisfying about making your own curry paste and, with your processor on standby, it takes less effort than opening a jar. You will certainly impress those lucky enough to sample your Malaysian lamb curry or prawn laksa. Try whizzing up a nut or herb crust to encase a tender beef or pork fillet, slather a spicy paste over a beautiful whole fish, or spread a smoky eggplant tapenade on crackers. Whether you're serving a quick mid-week meal for the family or something special when friends drop in, don't forget to tell them you made it from scratch, but don't tell them how easy it was — every cook is entitled to a few secrets.

parmesan-crusted lemon chicken

serves 4

crust

3 thick slices day-old **white bread**, crusts removed

25 g (1 oz/1/4 cup) grated **parmesan cheese**

grated **zest** of 2 **lemons**

100 g (31/2 oz/1 cup) **walnuts**

1 tablespoon **thyme**

1 tablespoon **rosemary**

1 small handful **oregano**

sea salt, to taste

60 g (21/4 oz/1/2 cup) **seasoned plain (all-purpose) flour**

2 **eggs**

4 boneless, skinless **chicken breasts**

lemon wedges, to serve

To make the crust, preheat the oven to 150°C (300°F/Gas 2). Cut the bread into chunks, spread on a baking tray and bake for 15–20 minutes, without browning, until completely dry. Cool, then transfer to a small processor fitted with the metal blade. Add the parmesan, lemon zest, walnuts, thyme, rosemary and oregano and whizz for 30 seconds, or until the mixture resembles fine breadcrumbs. Transfer to a large bowl and season with sea salt and freshly ground black pepper.

Increase the oven to 190°C (375°F/Gas 5). Put the seasoned flour in a bowl. Lightly whisk the eggs in another bowl. Coat each chicken breast with the flour, dip into the egg and then coat evenly with the breadcrumb mixture.

Put the crumbed chicken breasts on a baking tray lined with baking paper. Bake for 15 minutes, then turn and bake for a further 10 minutes, or until the chicken is cooked through.

Slice each chicken breast on the diagonal into four pieces and fan out on serving plates. Serve with lemon wedges.

tip The chicken can be crumbed in advance. Refrigerate, covered, for up to 2 hours before cooking.

tuna steaks with green olive paste

serves 4

olive paste
2 slices **white bread**, crusts removed

1 handful **flat-leaf (Italian) parsley**

2 teaspoons grated **lemon zest**

2 teaspoons **lemon juice**

1 **garlic clove**, chopped

80 g (2³/4 oz/2/3 cup) pitted **green olives**

1 tablespoon **olive oil**

4 x 185 g (6¹/2 oz) **tuna steaks**

2 tablespoons **lemon juice**

2 tablespoons **white wine**

80 g (2³/4 oz) **unsalted butter**

Preheat the oven to 200°C (400°F/Gas 6).

To make the olive paste, put the bread and parsley in a small processor fitted with the metal blade. Whizz for 30 seconds, or until the mixture forms breadcrumbs. Add the lemon zest, lemon juice, garlic and olives. Whizz for 10 seconds, or until the mixture comes together. With the motor running, slowly add the olive oil to form a smooth paste. Season well with salt and freshly ground black pepper.

Put the tuna steaks in an ovenproof dish. Spread some olive paste evenly over the tuna. Pour the lemon juice and wine around the tuna. Bake for 12–15 minutes, or until done to your liking. The tuna should still be pink in the centre.

Meanwhile, melt the butter in a saucepan over medium heat and cook until the butter turns a nut brown colour. Transfer the tuna to serving plates and drizzle with the melted butter.

tips The tuna is delicious served on a bed of potato mash. Store any leftover olive paste in an airtight container in the refrigerator for up to a week.

lamb cutlets with nut and orange crust

serves 4

paste

125 ml (4 fl oz/1/2 cup) **extra virgin olive oil**

1 large **onion**, roughly chopped

3 **garlic cloves**, roughly chhopped

juice of 1 **orange**

15 g (1/2 oz/1/2 bunch) **sage**

12 **lamb cutlets**

3 **eggs**, lightly beaten

light olive oil, for frying

lemon wedges, to serve

crust

35 g (11/4 oz/1/4 cup) **hazelnuts**

35 g (11/4 oz/1/4 cup) **pistachio kernels**

grated **zest** of 1 **orange**

6 thick slices **country-style white bread**, crusts removed, lightly toasted

large pinch of **sea salt**

To make the paste, put the oil, onion, garlic, orange juice and sage in a mini processor. Whizz for 45 seconds, or until well combined.

Put the lamb cutlets in a shallow non-metallic dish, spoon over the paste, cover and refrigerate for 2 hours, or overnight.

To make the crust, put the hazelnuts, pistachios, orange zest, half the bread and the sea salt in the processor and whizz in 3-second bursts for 1–11/2 minutes, or until the mixture resembles coarse breadcrumbs. Add the remaining bread and whizz in short bursts for 1 minute.

Remove the cutlets from the paste and set aside. Put the egg and crust mixture in separate shallow bowls. Dip the cutlets into the egg, shaking off the excess, and then coat in the crust mixture, turning them until completely coated.

Pour olive oil into a large non-stick frying pan to a depth of 5 mm (1/4 inch) and heat over medium–high heat. Fry the lamb cutlets in batches for 2–3 minutes each side, or until crunchy and golden. Drain on paper towels and keep warm while you cook the remaining cutlets. Serve with lemon wedges.

Put the **cutlets** in a shallow dish and spoon over the **paste**.

Dip the cutlets into the egg, then **coat** in the crust mixture, **turning** them until completely coated.

green masala on spatchcock

serves 4

masala

1/2 teaspoon **fenugreek seeds**

3 **cloves**

5 **coriander seeds**

5 **green cardamom pods**, bruised

2 **dried bird's eye chillies**

3 **garlic cloves**, crushed

1 teaspoon finely grated fresh **ginger**

1 handful **mint**

1 handful **coriander (cilantro) leaves**

1/2 small **green capsicum (pepper)**, seeded and chopped

1 1/2 tablespoons **cider vinegar**

1 teaspoon **ground turmeric**

1 teaspoon **salt**

1 1/2 tablespoons **vegetable oil**

1 1/2 tablespoons **sesame oil**

4 **spatchcocks (poussins)**

vegetable oil spray

To make the masala, put the fenugreek seeds in a small bowl, cover with water and set aside to soak overnight.

Drain the fenugreek seeds and dry on paper towels. Heat a dry heavy-based frying pan over medium–high heat and fry the cloves, coriander seeds and cardamom pods for 2–3 minutes, or until the spices are aromatic. Add the fenugreek seeds and stir for 10–15 seconds. Remove the mixture from the pan and set aside to cool. Transfer to a spice mill and whizz until finely ground.

Put the dried chillies, garlic, ginger, mint, coriander, capsicum and vinegar in a mini processor. Whizz in 5-second bursts for 20 seconds, or until puréed. Add the turmeric, salt and ground fenugreek mixture and briefly whizz to combine.

Heat the oils in a small frying pan over medium heat. Add the spice paste and fry for 15–20 seconds, or until the oil bubbles. Set aside to cool.

Dry the spatchcocks with paper towels. Remove the spines by cutting down both sides of the spine with poultry scissors. Put the spatchcocks on a board, breast side up, and press down firmly with your hand to butterfly them. Rub the masala paste all over the spatchcocks and put them in a shallow non-metallic dish. Cover and chill for 4 hours.

Heat the barbecue plate or chargrill pan to medium. Spray with oil and add the spatchcocks, skin side down. Fry for 8–10 minutes, or until the skin is crisp and golden. Turn the spatchcocks and fry for 5 minutes, or until cooked through. Serve hot or at room temperature.

tip Store the masala in an airtight container in the refrigerator for up to 10 days.

Soak the fenugreek seeds in a **bowl of water**.

Put the **chillies**, garlic, ginger, mint, coriander, capsicum and vinegar **in a processor**.

245

fiery thai red curry paste

makes 250 ml (9 fl oz/1 cup)

15 **long red chillies**

1/2 teaspoon **ground cumin**

3 **garlic cloves**, roughly chopped

3 large **red Asian shallots**, roughly chopped

1 tablespoon roughly chopped **galangal**

2 **makrut (kaffir lime) leaves**, shredded

2 **lemon grass stems**, white part only, sliced

4 **coriander (cilantro) roots** including 5 cm (2 inches) stems, roughly chopped

60 ml (2 fl oz/1/4 cup) **peanut oil**

1/2 teaspoon finely grated **lime zest**

1/4 teaspoon **salt**

Preheat the oven to 220°C (425°F/Gas 7). Line a baking tray with baking paper. Put the whole chillies on the baking tray and roast for 15 minutes, or until the skins start to blacken. Transfer to a plastic bag to cool for 10 minutes.

Meanwhile, heat a small, dry, non-stick frying pan over medium heat. Add the cumin and cook for 2 minutes, or until aromatic. Remove from the pan.

Wearing disposable gloves, remove and discard the chilli stalks and skins. Put the chillies in a small processor fitted with the metal blade and add the garlic and shallots. Whizz for 15 seconds, or until evenly chopped.

Add the galangal, lime leaves, lemon grass, coriander roots and stems, oil, lime zest, salt and cumin. Season with freshly ground black pepper. Whizz for 1 minute, or until finely chopped. Add 1 teaspoon of water at a time until the mixture reaches a spreadable consistency. Whizz to combine.

tips Use 2–3 tablespoons of the paste for a vegetable or chicken curry to serve four people. Store the paste in an airtight container in the refrigerator for up to 3 weeks, or spoon into ice cube trays and freeze.

247

beef with hot and spicy curry paste

serves 4

paste

6 **dried long red chillies**

4 **red Asian shallots**, roughly chopped

4 **garlic cloves**, roughly chopped

3 **lemon grass stems**, white part only,
   roughly chopped

3 teaspoons grated fresh **ginger**

1 teaspoon **ground coriander**

1 teaspoon **ground cumin**

6 **coriander (cilantro) roots**

2 teaspoons **shrimp paste**

2 1/2 tablespoons **roasted peanuts**

2 tablespoons **vegetable oil**

800 g (1 lb 12 oz) **beef fillet**

2 tablespoons **olive oil**

145 ml (4 3/4 fl oz) **coconut milk**

To make the paste, put the chillies in a small bowl. Cover with warm water and soak for 10 minutes. Discard the water and roughly chop the chillies. Put the chillies in a mini processor and add the shallots, garlic, lemon grass, ginger, ground coriander, cumin, coriander roots, shrimp paste, peanuts and oil. Whizz for 1 1/2–2 minutes, or until the mixture forms a smooth paste. Add a little water if necessary.

Tie the piece of beef with kitchen string at regular intervals to help keep its shape. Rub 80 ml (2 1/2 fl oz/1/3 cup) of the paste all over the beef and refrigerate for 1 hour.

Preheat the oven to 190°C (375°F/Gas 5). Heat the olive oil in a flameproof casserole dish over medium–high heat and add the beef. Fry briefly for 6–8 minutes, or until brown all over. Pour the coconut milk around the beef. Cover the dish and bake for 15 minutes for rare beef, or until done to your liking. Remove the beef from the dish, loosely cover with foil and set aside to rest for 10 minutes.

Reheat the sauce on the stovetop just before serving. Slice the beef and serve with the sauce.

tips Naan bread and basmati rice are ideal accompaniments to this dish. Store any leftover paste, covered, in the refrigerator for up to a week. It can also be frozen for later use.

chicken with herb pangrattato

serves 4

herb pangrattato

4 slices day-old **white bread**, crusts removed

1 teaspoon **dried oregano**

2 tablespoons chopped **oregano**

2 tablespoons chopped **basil**

2 teaspoons grated **lemon zest**

1/2 teaspoon freshly ground **black pepper**

4 boneless, skinless **chicken breasts**

4 slices **prosciutto**

12 **sage leaves**

plain (all-purpose) flour, for coating

1 **egg**, lightly beaten

2 tablespoons **light olive oil**

lemon wedges, to serve

sage leaves, to serve

To make the herb pangrattato, put the bread slices in a small processor fitted with the metal blade. Whizz for 30 seconds, or until breadcrumbs form. Add the dried and fresh oregano, basil, lemon zest and pepper and whizz until well combined.

Slice through the thick part of each chicken breast, without cutting all the way through, and open out. Cover the chicken breasts with plastic wrap and use a meat mallet to gently and evenly flatten them until they are 1 cm (1/2 inch) thick. Lay a slice of prosciutto and three sage leaves over each chicken breast. Roll up from the long side and secure with toothpicks.

Put the flour, egg and herb pangrattato in separate bowls. Coat each chicken roll with the flour, dip into the egg and then roll in the pangrattato. Refrigerate for at least 20 minutes.

Preheat the oven to 180°C (350°F/Gas 4). Heat the oil in a heavy-based frying pan over medium heat. Add the chicken rolls and fry for 5 minutes on each side, or until golden. Transfer the rolls to a baking tray and bake for 10 minutes, or until the chicken is cooked through. Remove the toothpicks and set aside for 5 minutes before serving. Thickly slice each chicken roll on the diagonal, pile onto plates and serve with lemon wedges and sage leaves.

tip The chicken rolls can be coated with the pangrattato several hours ahead. Cover and chill until needed.

Slice each chicken breast through the **thick part**, without **cutting** all the way through.

Lay the **prosciutto** and sage leaves over the chicken, then **roll up** and secure with toothpicks.

dukkah

makes 100 g (3¹/2 oz/³/4 cup)

30 g (1 oz/¹/4 cup) **roasted skinned hazelnuts**

50 g (1³/4 oz/¹/3 cup) **toasted sesame seeds** (see tips)

2 tablespoons **coriander seeds**

2 teaspoons **cumin seeds**

1 teaspoon **fennel seeds**

¹/2 teaspoon freshly ground **black pepper**

¹/4 teaspoon **sea salt**

Preheat the oven to 200°C (400°F/Gas 6). Whizz the hazelnuts in a spice mill or mini processor for 12 seconds, or until roughly ground, taking care not to overprocess the nuts or they will form a paste. Don't worry if the nuts are chopped unevenly, with some chunky pieces. Transfer the nuts to a bowl and add the sesame seeds.

Fry the coriander seeds in a small, dry, non-stick frying pan over medium heat for 7–8 minutes, or until aromatic. Remove from the pan. Repeat with the cumin seeds and then the fennel seeds in separate batches, cooking each for 2–3 minutes, or until fragrant.

Transfer the spices to the spice mill or processor and whizz for 10 seconds, or until finely chopped. Add to the hazelnut mixture, along with the pepper and salt, and mix well to combine. When completely cool, transfer to an airtight container.

tips Toasted sesame seeds are available from Asian stores. Serve the dukkah as a dip with pitta bread and extra virgin olive oil, or use to crumb chicken or to sprinkle over salads or roasted vegetables.

255

lamb with malaysian curry paste

serves 4

paste

1 **red onion**, chopped

2 tablespoons **madras curry paste** or **mild curry paste**

1 tablespoon **soy sauce**

1 small **red chilli**, seeded and chopped

10 cm (4 inch) piece of **lemon grass**, finely chopped

2¹/2 teaspoons grated fresh **ginger**

2 **garlic cloves**, chopped

4 **makrut (kaffir lime) leaves**, roughly chopped or torn

2 tablespoons **tomato paste (concentrated purée)**

800 g (1 lb 12 oz) diced **lamb**

2 tablespoons **oil**

1 **onion**, halved and thinly sliced

400 ml (14 fl oz) **coconut milk**

200 ml (7 fl oz) **vegetable stock**

1 **small red chilli**, sliced, to garnish

1 **kaffir lime leaf**, sliced, to garnish

coriander (cilantro) sprigs, to garnish

Combine the diced lamb and half the **curry paste** and marinate for 1 hour.

Add the **coconut milk** and stock to the lamb mixture in **the saucepan**.

To make the paste, put the onion, curry paste, soy sauce, chilli, lemon grass and ginger in a small processor fitted with the metal blade. Whizz for 30 seconds, or until the mixture has a coarse texture. Add the garlic, lime leaves, tomato paste and 1 tablespoon of water and whizz until smooth.

Put the diced lamb in a bowl and add half the curry paste. Mix well and refrigerate for 1 hour.

Heat the oil in a large saucepan over medium heat and add the onion. Fry, stirring regularly, for 5 minutes. Remove the onion from the saucepan. Increase the heat to high, add half the lamb and fry for 5 minutes, or until browned on all sides. Transfer to a bowl and brown the remaining lamb.

Return all of the lamb and onion to the saucepan, add the coconut milk and stock and stir well. Bring to the boil, then reduce the heat and simmer, covered, for 45 minutes, or until the lamb is very tender. Remove the lid and simmer for 10 minutes, or until the sauce is slightly thickened. Serve garnished with chilli, lime leaf and coriander.

tip Steamed rice is an ideal accompaniment to this dish. Store the remaining curry paste, covered, in the refrigerator for up to a week. Alternatively, freeze it for later use.

aromatic yoghurt paste for chicken or fish

makes 250 ml (9 fl oz/1 cup)

4 **spring onions (scallions)**, roughly chopped

2 **garlic cloves**, roughly chopped

2¹/2 tablespoons grated fresh **ginger**

1 **green chilli**, chopped

1/2 teaspoon **ground coriander**

1/2 teaspoon **ground cumin**

200 g (7 oz/³/4 cup) **Greek-style yoghurt**

1 tablespoon **lemon juice**

Put the spring onion, garlic, ginger and chilli in a mini processor and whizz for 30 seconds, or until finely chopped. Add the coriander, cumin and half the yoghurt and whizz until smooth.

Transfer the paste to a non-metallic bowl. Add the remaining yoghurt and the lemon juice and mix well.

tips Use the paste to rub on pieces of chicken or fish for 2–3 hours before barbecuing, grilling (broiling) or baking. There is sufficient paste for 800 g (1 lb 12 oz) of chicken or fish. Store the paste, covered, in the refrigerator for up to a week.

roast beef with mushroom and rosemary rub

serves 4

rub

15 g (1/2 oz) **dried porcini mushrooms**

3 tablespoons **rosemary leaves**

1 teaspoon **cumin seeds**

1 teaspoon **coriander seeds**

1/4 teaspoon **salt**

4-rib **standing beef rib roast**,
    at least 1 kg (2 lb 4 oz)

1 teaspoon **olive oil**

55 g (2 oz) **butter**

250 ml (9 fl oz/1 cup) **dry white wine**

rosemary sprigs, to garnish

To make the rub, put the mushrooms, rosemary, cumin seeds, coriander seeds and salt in a spice mill and whizz for 30 seconds, or until finely chopped. The rosemary can be a little coarser than the rest of the mixture.

Dry the beef with paper towels. Rub the oil all over the surface, then cover with the mushroom mixture, rubbing it in well. Set aside to rest for 30 minutes.

Preheat the oven to 230°C (450°F/Gas 8). Sit the beef on a roasting rack in a roasting tin. Dot the butter over the top and roast for 20 minutes. Reduce the oven to 170°C (325°F/Gas 3), loosely cover the top of the beef with foil and pour the wine into the tin. Roast for 30 minutes for medium–rare, or until done to your liking.

Transfer the beef, still covered with foil, to a carving plate and return it to the oven. Turn off the oven and leave the door slightly ajar. Transfer the roasting tin to the stovetop and simmer over medium heat for 1 1/2–2 minutes, or until the juices have reduced and thickened slightly. Season with salt and freshly ground black pepper.

Carve the beef between the ribs and serve drizzled with the pan juices. Garnish with rosemary sprigs.

north african spiced fish parcels

serves 4

2 large **all-purpose potatoes**, washed, unpeeled

olive oil, for brushing

4 x 220 g (7³/4 oz) thick skinless **blue eye cod fillets** or **snapper fillets**

2 **vine-ripened tomatoes**, thinly sliced lengthways

paste

1 small **onion**, roughly chopped

2 **garlic cloves**

1 **dried red chilli**, crumbled

2 teaspoons **cumin seeds**

1 teaspoon **sweet paprika**

1 handful **flat-leaf (Italian) parsley**

1 handful **coriander (cilantro) leaves**

4 **anchovy fillets**

grated **zest** and **juice** of 1 **lemon**

80 ml (2¹/2 fl oz/¹/3 cup) **extra virgin olive oil**

salad greens, to serve

Parboil the **potatoes**,
then **slice** them lengthways.

Brush the spice paste all
over the **fish fillets**.

Parboil the potatoes in boiling salted water for 10 minutes. Drain and set aside to cool for 15 minutes. Cut each potato lengthways into six slices.

Preheat the oven to 200°C (400°F/Gas 6). Line a baking sheet with baking paper. Cut four 30 cm (12 inch) squares of baking paper and foil. Put the baking paper squares on top of the foil squares and brush the centre of each with oil. Set aside.

To make the paste, put the onion, garlic, chilli, cumin seeds and paprika in a mini processor. Whizz for 1 minute, or until a coarse paste forms. Add the parsley, coriander, anchovies, lemon zest, lemon juice and oil and whizz for 40 seconds, or until evenly chopped.

Brush the paste all over the fish fillets, coating them thoroughly.

Divide the potato and tomato slices among the prepared foil and paper squares, making an even layer on each. Season with salt and freshly ground black pepper and top with the fish fillets. Pull one side of each square over the top of the fish to meet the opposite side. Fold the edges over tightly to seal the parcels. Put the parcels on the prepared baking sheet and bake for 25 minutes.

Break the parcels open with a sharp knife. Using a large spatula, transfer the fish and vegetables to plates and serve immediately, accompanied with salad greens.

beef in indian spice paste

serves 4

paste

1/2 teaspoon **cardamom seeds**

1 teaspoon **ajowan seeds** (see tips)

1 teaspoon **cumin seeds**

11/2 teaspoons **black peppercorns**

1 teaspoon **salt**

2 **bird's eye chillies**, seeded

1 tablespoon finely chopped fresh
   ginger

1 small **onion**, roughly chopped

3 **garlic cloves**

1 tablespoon **lemon juice**

250 g (9 oz/1 cup) **Greek-style yoghurt**

1.25 kg (2 lb 12 oz) **beef eye fillet**
   (thick end)

To make the paste, put the cardamom, ajowan, cumin, peppercorns and salt in a mini processor. Whizz for 20 seconds, or until roughly chopped. Add the chillies, ginger, onion and garlic and whizz until the mixture forms a rough paste. Transfer to a small bowl and stir in the lemon juice and yoghurt.

Tie the beef fillet in three to four places with kitchen string to give a thick, even log. Put the beef in a large roasting tin and thickly coat all over with the paste. Cover and refrigerate for 2 hours, or overnight.

Preheat the oven to 220°C (425°F/Gas 7). Bring the beef to room temperature while the oven is heating. Bake the beef for 35 minutes. Cover the roasting tin with a double layer of foil and set aside to rest in a warm place for 15 minutes. Transfer the beef to a chopping board and cut into 5 mm (1/4 inch) slices.

tips Ajowan or carum is a north Indian spice with a flavour similar to thyme and a peppery aftertaste. It is sold in speciality grocery stores. You could ask your butcher to tie the beef fillet with the string. The beef goes well with boiled potatoes that have been tossed with olive oil and coriander (cilantro), or a herb and fennel salad.

prawn laksa

serves 4

laksa paste

1 teaspoon **coriander seeds**

1/2 teaspoon **cumin seeds**

1 **onion**, roughly chopped

1 tablespoon grated fresh **ginger**

1 tablespoon grated **galangal**

2 **lemon grass stems**, white part only, thinly sliced

3 **garlic cloves**

4 **bird's eye chillies**, sliced

5 **candlenuts** (see tip, page 272)

1 tablespoon **shrimp paste** (see tip, page 272)

2 **coriander (cilantro) roots**, finely chopped

1 teaspoon **ground turmeric**

1 teaspoon **ground coriander**

1 teaspoon **ground cumin**

80 ml (2 1/2 fl oz/1/3 cup) **peanut oil**

1 litre (35 fl oz/4 cups) **chicken stock**

400 ml (14 fl oz) **coconut milk**

1 tablespoon shaved **palm sugar** or **soft brown sugar**

1 tablespoon **fish sauce**

2 tablespoons **lime juice**

6 **fried tofu puffs**, cut in half diagonally

16 **raw prawns (shrimp)**, peeled and deveined, leaving the tails intact

3 **makrut (kaffir lime) leaves**, finely shredded

8 **snow peas (mangetout)**, sliced lengthways on the diagonal

200 g (7 oz) **rice vermicelli**

90 g (3 1/4 oz/1 cup) **bean sprouts**, trimmed

1 **Lebanese (short) cucumber**, cut into matchsticks

1 handful **coriander (cilantro) leaves**, plus extra to serve

1 handful **mint**

2 **bird's eye chillies**, thinly sliced

2 tablespoons **fried shallots** (see tip, page 272)

To make the laksa paste, put the coriander and cumin seeds in a small dry frying pan and fry over medium–high heat for 1–2 minutes, or until aromatic. Transfer to a spice mill and whizz for 45 seconds, or until the seeds form a coarse powder. Transfer the seeds to a small processor fitted with the metal blade and add the onion, ginger, galangal, lemon grass, garlic, chilli, candlenuts, shrimp paste, coriander roots, ground turmeric, ground coriander, ground cumin and oil. Whizz for 2 minutes, or until the mixture forms a paste.

Put the laksa paste in a large heavy-based saucepan over medium–high heat and fry, stirring constantly, for 5–6 minutes, or until fragrant. Reduce the heat to medium and add the stock, coconut milk, sugar and fish sauce. Slowly bring to the boil, stirring constantly. Add the lime juice, tofu puffs, prawns, lime leaves and snow peas and simmer for 2–3 minutes, or until the prawns turn pink.

Meanwhile, cook the rice vermicelli according to the manufacturer's instructions.

Divide the vermicelli among four large bowls, then spoon the tofu puffs, prawns and snow peas on top. Add the hot soup and top with the bean sprouts and cucumber. Sprinkle with the coriander, mint, chilli and fried shallots. Serve topped with coriander leaves.

tip Candlenuts, shrimp paste and fried shallots are available from Asian grocery stores and larger supermarkets.

Fry the **coriander** and **cumin seeds** in a small dry frying pan **until aromatic**.

Whizz the seeds and remaining ingredients until the mixture forms a **paste**.

island baked snapper

serves 4

paste

235 g (8¹/2 oz/4 cups) **shredded coconut**

1 **green papaya**

grated **zest** of 2 **limes**

125 ml (4 fl oz/¹/2 cup) **lime juice**

400 ml (14 fl oz) **coconut milk**

sea salt, to taste

2 kg (4 lb 8 oz) **whole snapper**, scaled and cleaned

lime wedges, to serve

To make the paste, preheat the oven to 180°C (350°F/Gas 4). Divide the shredded coconut between two shallow baking tins lined with baking paper and toast for 10–15 minutes, or until golden.

Halve the papaya lengthways, scrape out the seeds and peel the flesh. Roughly chop the papaya and put in a small processor fitted with the metal blade. Whizz for 15 seconds, or until finely chopped. Transfer to a large bowl.

Add the toasted coconut, lime zest, lime juice and coconut milk to the processor and whizz for 15–20 seconds, or until semi-smooth. Add to the papaya and season with sea salt.

Lightly rinse the cavity of the snapper and dry the fish with paper towels. Put the fish in a roasting tin lined with baking paper. Smother both sides of the fish with the paste. Cover with foil and refrigerate for 1 hour.

Preheat the oven to 190°C (375°F/Gas 5). Remove the foil and bake the fish for 40–45 minutes, or until cooked through. Serve whole on a platter, accompanied by lime wedges.

pork steaks with a nut crust

serves 4

crust

80 g (2¾ oz/½ cup) **roasted macadamia nuts**

2 slices day-old **white bread**, toasted, crusts removed

1 small handful **sage**

1 slice **prosciutto**, roughly chopped

1 teaspoon grated **lemon zest**

½ **red apple**, unpeeled, roughly chopped

pinch of **cayenne pepper**

20 g (¾ oz) **butter**, melted

40 g (1½ oz/⅓ cup) **seasoned plain (all-purpose) flour**

1 **egg**, lightly beaten

4 **butterflied pork loin steaks**

20 g (¾ oz) **butter**

2 tablespoons **oil**

sage leaves, to serve (see tip, page 279)

lemon wedges, to serve

Put the **macadamia** nuts, bread, sage and **prosciutto** in a small processor fitted with the metal blade.

Add the lemon zest, apple, cayenne pepper and **melted butter** to the macadamia mixture.

To make the crust, put the macadamia nuts, bread, sage and prosciutto in a small processor fitted with the metal blade. Whizz in 3-second bursts for 15–20 seconds, or until roughly combined. Add the lemon zest, chopped apple, cayenne pepper and melted butter and whizz for 6–8 seconds, or until the mixture forms a paste. Transfer to a plate.

Put the seasoned flour and egg in separate bowls. Lightly coat the pork steaks with the flour, dip into the egg, shaking off the excess, then press into the nut mixture, coating all over. Put the pork steaks on a plate, cover with plastic wrap and chill for 30–45 minutes.

Heat the butter and oil in a large non-stick frying pan over medium heat. Add the pork steaks and fry for 3–4 minutes each side, or until the crust is golden brown. Set aside to rest in a warm place for 2–3 minutes.

Serve the pork topped with sage leaves and accompanied by lemon wedges.

tip The sage leaves may be fried in a little butter until crisp.

mushroom pâté on crostini

serves 4

4 slices **white bread**, crusts removed

1 tablespoon **olive oil**

1 **onion**, chopped

2 **garlic cloves**, chopped

325 g (11 1/2 oz) **flat mushrooms**, chopped

125 ml (4 fl oz/1/2 cup) **white wine**

2 tablespoons **thyme**

4 tablespoons chopped **parsley**

2 tablespoons **lemon juice**, or to taste

1 tablespoon **pouring cream**

crostini

1 small **baguette**, thinly sliced on the diagonal

olive oil spray

2 **garlic cloves**, halved

Cook the **onion** and **garlic** in a deep-sided frying pan.

Add the mushrooms, wine and thyme to the **onion mixture** and **simmer** for 10 minutes.

Whizz the bread in a small processor fitted with the metal blade for 20 seconds, or until it forms breadcrumbs. You will need 80 g (2³/4 oz/1 cup) of breadcrumbs.

Heat the oil in a deep-sided frying pan over medium heat. Add the onion and garlic and cook for 2 minutes. Add the mushrooms, wine and thyme, cover and simmer, stirring once or twice, for 10 minutes. Remove the lid and allow any liquid to evaporate. Set aside to cool a little.

Put the mushroom mixture, breadcrumbs, parsley, lemon juice and cream in the processor and whizz for 30 seconds, or until finely chopped. Add more lemon juice, to taste, and season well with salt and freshly ground black pepper. Cover and refrigerate for at least 1 hour.

To make the crostini, preheat the oven to 180°C (350°F/Gas 4). Lightly spray each side of the baguette slices with oil and arrange on a large baking tray. Bake, turning once, for 12–15 minutes, or until crisp and golden. Rub each crostini with the cut surface of the garlic.

Serve the crostini spread with the mushroom pâté.

tip Store the pâté, covered, in the refrigerator for up to 5 days.

smoky eggplant tapenade

makes 750 ml (26 fl oz/3 cups)

1 **eggplant (aubergine)**, about 500 g (1 lb 2 oz)

290 g (10¼ oz/2 cups) pitted **kalamata olives**

5 **anchovy fillets**

35 g (1¼ oz/¼ cup) **capers**, rinsed and squeezed dry

3 **garlic cloves**, finely chopped

1 small handful **flat-leaf (Italian) parsley**

1 small handful **basil**

1 small handful **oregano**

1 tablespoon **lemon juice**

1 tablespoon **extra virgin olive oil**

Preheat the barbecue chargrill plate to high. Cook the eggplant, turning frequently, for 15–20 minutes, or until the skin is black all over and the flesh is soft. Remove from the heat. When cool enough to handle, cut off the stem, peel off the skin and roughly chop the eggplant flesh.

Put the olives, anchovies, capers, garlic, parsley, basil, oregano, lemon juice and oil in a small processor fitted with the metal blade. Whizz for 10–15 seconds, or until roughly chopped.

Add the chopped eggplant and whizz in 3-second bursts for 15 seconds, or until the tapenade has a medium–smooth consistency with a little texture. Season with freshly ground black pepper and transfer to a serving bowl.

tips The tapenade is delicious served with crackers, barbecued lamb fillets or chargrilled tuna. Store in an airtight container in the refrigerator for up to 3 weeks. If you have a gas stove, you can place the eggplant directly on the open flame and follow the same cooking process as chargrilling. This will take half the time and give an even smokier flavour.

roasted capsicum, chilli and semi-dried tomato spread

makes 500 ml (17 fl oz/2 cups)

1 large **red capsicum (pepper)**, seeded and quartered

90 g (3¼ oz/½ cup) **semi-dried (sun-blushed) tomatoes**

2 teaspoons **sambal oelek**

125 g (4½ oz/½ cup) **spreadable cream cheese**

2 tablespoons chopped **basil**

Preheat the grill (broiler) to high. Arrange the capsicum, skin side up, on a wire rack and grill (broil) for 10 minutes, or until well blackened. Cool in a plastic bag, then peel and discard the skin. Chop the flesh.

Drain the semi-dried tomatoes well on paper towels, pat dry and roughly chop. Put in a small processor fitted with the metal blade and add the capsicum, sambal oelek, cream cheese and basil. Whizz for 10 seconds, or until roughly combined. The tomatoes should still have some texture. Season well with salt and freshly ground black pepper.

tips Serve the spread on toasted pitta bread fingers, or other breads and biscuits. It also goes well with boiled or roasted new potatoes. Store the spread, covered, in the refrigerator for up to 5 days.

roast garlic and artichoke spread on piadini

serves 4

piadini

250 g (9 oz/2 cups) **plain (all-purpose) flour**

60 ml (2 fl oz/1/4 cup) **milk**

60 ml (2 fl oz/1/4 cup) **olive oil**

1 teaspoon **salt**

spread

1 **garlic bulb**

olive oil spray

400 g (14 oz) tin **artichoke hearts in brine**, drained

3 tablespoons chopped **flat-leaf (Italian) parsley**

2 tablespoons **olive oil**

Turn out the dough and **knead** on a floured surface until **smooth and elastic**.

Roll each piece of dough into a **thin disc**.

To make the piadini, put the flour in a small processor fitted with the plastic blade. Add the milk, oil, salt and 80 ml (2½ fl oz/⅓ cup) of water. Whizz until a smooth, slightly sticky ball forms, adding a little more water if needed. Turn out onto a floured surface and knead for 10 minutes, or until smooth and elastic.

Cut the dough into three pieces. Cover with plastic wrap and set aside for at least 20 minutes. Roll each piece of dough into a 23 cm (9 inch) disc, 2 mm (1/16 inch) thick.

Slowly heat a large cast-iron skillet or heavy-based frying pan over low heat until very hot. Add one of the dough discs and cook for 20 seconds, then turn and cook the other side for 20 seconds. Prick all over four or five times, then cook, turning frequently, for a further 3–4 minutes, or until the dough is dry and white, but mottled with burn marks. Transfer to a wire rack to cool. Repeat with the remaining dough discs.

Meanwhile, to make the spread, preheat the oven to 180°C (350°F/Gas 4). Spray the garlic with oil, then wrap in foil. Bake for 30 minutes, or until soft. Set aside to cool, then squeeze the garlic flesh into a bowl.

Gently squeeze the excess water from the artichokes, then cut them in half. Pat the artichokes dry with paper towels and spray well with oil. Heat a chargrill pan to very hot. Add the artichokes and cook, turning often, for 2–3 minutes, or until browned.

Put the artichokes, garlic purée, parsley and oil in the processor fitted with the metal blade. Season well with salt and freshly ground black pepper and whizz for 12–15 seconds, or until roughly blended.

Cut the piadini into wedges and coat thickly with the spread.

tip The piadini can be reheated in a 200°C (400°F/Gas 6) oven for 5 minutes.

creamy baccala and garlic spread

makes 500 ml (17 fl oz/2 cups)

400 g (14 oz) **salt cod (baccala)** (see tips)

125 ml (4 fl oz/1/2 cup) **olive oil**

2 **garlic cloves**, roughly chopped

150 ml (5 fl oz) **pouring cream**

juice of 1/2 **lemon**

1/2 teaspoon **thyme**

freshly ground **white pepper**, to taste

Put the salt cod in a large, shallow dish and cover with plenty of cold water. Cover with plastic wrap and refrigerate for 2 days, changing the water twice a day.

Drain the salt cod and rinse again. Put in a large saucepan, cover with cold water and slowly heat over medium–low heat until nearly boiling. Cook, with just a few bubbles appearing, for 10 minutes. Try to prevent the water from boiling as this will toughen the cod. Drain and rinse under cold water until cold enough to handle. Remove the skin and bones, being careful to leave no bones in the flesh.

Meanwhile, heat the oil and garlic in a small saucepan over low heat for 3–4 minutes, or until the garlic becomes aromatic. Remove from the heat.

Put the salt cod in a small processor fitted with the metal blade and add the garlic. Whizz for 25–30 seconds, or until smooth. With the motor running, slowly add the oil. Add the cream and whizz in 5-second bursts until combined. Add the lemon juice, thyme and freshly ground white pepper, to taste, and whizz for 2–3 seconds, or until just combined.

tips Where possible, select fleshy pieces of salt cod rather than whole salted and dry cod — it's easier to handle and there's less wastage. Serve the spread with melba toasts or crispbreads, garnished with thyme sprigs. Store, covered, in the refrigerator for up to 3 days. Stir in a little warm cream to serve.

smoked salmon brandade with turkish toast

serves 4–6

pide (Turkish/flat bread), to serve

olive oil spray

brandade

2 small (200 g/7 oz) **potatoes**, cut into 5 cm (2 inch) pieces

2 tablespoons **olive oil**

1/2 small **red onion**, chopped

2 **garlic cloves**, chopped

1 tablespoon **capers**, rinsed and squeezed dry

125 g (41/2 oz) **smoked salmon**, roughly chopped

2 tablespoons chopped **dill**

2 tablespoons **pouring cream**

1 teaspoon grated **lemon zest**

1 tablespoon **lemon juice**

Preheat the oven to 180°C (350°F/Gas 4). Cut the bread into serving-sized pieces and split each horizontally. Lightly spray the cut sides with oil and arrange on a large baking tray. Toast for 12–15 minutes, or until crisp and golden.

To make the brandade, cook the potato cubes in a saucepan of boiling water for 8–10 minutes, or until tender. Drain and roughly chop with a flat-bladed knife.

Heat the oil in a small saucepan over low heat. Add the onion, garlic and capers and fry for 2–3 minutes. Transfer to a small processor fitted with the metal blade and add the warm potato and the salmon. Whizz in 2-second bursts for 15–20 seconds, or until roughly combined. Add the dill, cream, lemon zest and lemon juice. Season well with salt and freshly ground black pepper. Whizz for 10 seconds, or until the mixture is combined but still has some texture.

Serve the brandade spread on the toast.

tip Store the brandade, covered, in the refrigerator for up to 4 days. Bring to room temperature before serving.

Roughly chop the cooked
potato cubes.

Fry the red onion, garlic and
capers over **low heat**.

la capriata

serves 4

150 g (5¹/2 oz/1 cup) **dried broad (fava) beans**

4 **garlic cloves**

1 tablespoon **rosemary**, roughly chopped

2 teaspoons **tomato paste (concentrated purée)**

pinch of **cayenne pepper**

1 tablespoon **lemon juice**

60 ml (2 fl oz/1/4 cup) **extra virgin olive oil**

1/4 teaspoon **sesame oil**

extra **cayenne pepper**, to serve

Put the broad beans in a large bowl and cover with cold water. Leave to soak overnight, uncovered. Drain, rinse under cold water and put in a large saucepan with two of the garlic cloves. Cover with plenty of cold water and bring to the boil. Reduce the heat to low and simmer for 1 hour, or until tender.

Drain the broad beans and transfer to a blender or small processor fitted with the metal blade. Chop the remaining garlic cloves and add to the processor, along with the rosemary, tomato paste, cayenne pepper and lemon juice. Whizz for 12–15 seconds, or until finely chopped. Add the oils and whizz to combine, then season well with salt and freshly ground black pepper. Spoon into a serving dish, cover and chill for 24 hours.

Remove the spread from the refrigerator and bring to room temperature. Sprinkle the surface with cayenne pepper.

tip Serve the spread on pitta bread triangles.

mousses, terrines and starters

whizz to impress

So you'd like to impress with a special starter, but don't have the time? Try a smooth and subtle asparagus mousse, whizzed up in 20 minutes, or individual chicken, pancetta and pine nut terrines, made the day before when time was less pressing. For lunch? Perhaps Shanghai pork sticks served on lemon grass stems, or a colourful loaf of feta and ricotta cheeses wrapped in prosciutto. There are some beautiful recipes to choose from — some to be served hot on cool autumn evenings, others cold for simmering summer days. Some with that unmistakable French touch, others with delicate Asian flavours, but all are quickly and easily achieved by whizzing.

snapper, scallop and dill terrine

serves 12

50 g (1 3/4 oz) **butter**

500 g (1 lb 2 oz) skinless **snapper fillets**

12 large **scallops**

250 g (9 oz/1 cup) **cottage cheese**

1 tablespoon **lemon juice**

2 **eggs**

2 **egg whites**

3 tablespoons chopped **dill**

1 small handful **dill sprigs**, to serve

2–3 tablespoons **pink salmon roe**, to serve

1/2 **baguette**, thinly sliced, to serve

Preheat the oven to 170°C (325°F/Gas 3). Lightly spray a 1 litre (35 fl oz/4 cup) capacity loaf (bar) tin with oil and line with baking paper.

Melt the butter in a large frying pan, add the snapper and fry gently for 3 minutes. Add the scallops and cook for 2 minutes, turning them halfway through. Remove the pan from the heat and set aside to cool.

Transfer the cooled seafood to a processor fitted with the metal blade and add the cottage cheese, lemon juice, eggs and egg whites. Whizz for 12 seconds, or until smooth. Add the chopped dill and whizz in 3-second bursts for 9–12 seconds, or until the mixture is flecked with green.

Carefully spread the mixture into the prepared tin and put the loaf tin in a roasting tin. Pour in enough boiling water to come halfway up the sides of the tin and bake for 45–50 minutes, or until the terrine is firm and a skewer inserted into the centre comes out clean.

Leave the terrine in the water until cold, then remove from the water, cover with plastic wrap and chill for 2 hours.

Briefly dip the tin in hot water and invert the terrine onto a board. Garnish with the dill sprigs and salmon roe. Cut into slices to serve.

chicken galantine

serves 4–6

100 g (3¹/2 oz) **minced (ground) chicken**

150 g (5¹/2 oz) **minced (ground) pork**

1 teaspoon **green peppercorns**

170 ml (5¹/2 fl oz/²/3 cup) **Calvados** or **apple brandy**

2 tablespoons **pouring cream**

¹/2 teaspoon **mixed (pumpkin pie) spice**

1 **egg**

50 g (1³/4 oz) thickly sliced lean **ham**, cut into 1 cm (¹/2 inch) dice

35 g (1¹/4 oz/¹/4 cup) **pistachio kernels**

2 kg (4 lb 8 oz) **chicken**, boned (see tip, page 309)

80 g (2³/4 oz) **butter**, softened

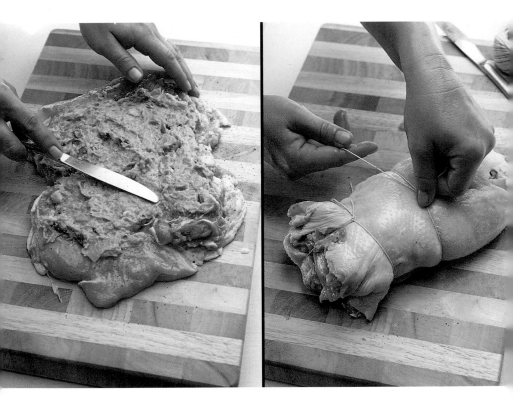

Spread the chicken and pork mixture over the **boned chicken,** leaving a border.

Tie the rolled chicken with **kitchen string** to help **keep its shape** during baking.

Preheat the oven to 170°C (325°F/Gas 3).

Put the chicken, pork and peppercorns in a small processor fitted with the metal blade. Whizz in 5-second bursts for 35–45 seconds, or until fine. Add 2 tablespoons of the Calvados or apple brandy, the cream, mixed spice and egg and season with salt and pepper. Whizz in short bursts until just combined. Remove the bowl from the machine and stir in the ham and pistachios.

Lay the chicken on a board, skin side down, ensuring that all the flesh is on top of the skin. Season with salt and pepper. Spread the chicken and pork mixture on top, leaving a 3 cm (1¼ inch) border. Roll the chicken into a fat log, tucking in the ends as you roll. Tie the chicken in three to four places with kitchen string to help keep its shape, then secure the seams with short skewers.

Rub the butter all over the skin and put the chicken on a wire rack in a roasting tin. Cover the tin with foil, sealing the edges tightly. Bake for 35 minutes.

Remove the foil and pour the remaining Calvados or brandy over the chicken. Bake for 50 minutes, basting with the pan juices every 15 minutes. Remove from the oven and set aside to cool, basting once or twice. Wrap the chicken in foil and refrigerate overnight. Cut into thin slices to serve.

tip Ask your butcher to bone the chicken for you, and to remove the bones without puncturing the skin.

steamed pork and prawn mousse in lettuce leaves

serves 4

400 g (14 oz) **raw prawns (shrimp)**, peeled and deveined

200 g (7 oz) **minced (ground) pork**

1/2 teaspoon chopped **coriander (cilantro) stems**

1 **garlic clove**, minced

1/2 teaspoon minced **ginger**

2 tablespoons **fish sauce**

185 ml (6 fl oz/3/4 cup) **coconut milk**

2 **eggs**

4 large **lettuce leaves**

1/4 **red chilli**, shredded

1 **makrut (kaffir lime) leaf**, shredded

2–3 **lettuce leaves**, extra, for steaming

extra shredded **red chilli**, to serve

extra shredded **makrut (kaffir lime) leaf**, to serve

Put the prawns, pork, coriander, garlic, ginger and fish sauce in a small processor fitted with the metal blade. Whizz for 40 seconds, or until the mixture forms a paste. With the motor running, gradually add the coconut milk. Add the eggs and whizz until just combined.

Lay the lettuce leaves on a flat surface. Spoon one-quarter of the prawn and pork paste in a pile on the centre of each lettuce leaf. Sprinkle with the chilli and lime leaf, then tightly fold the lettuce leaves over the filling to make a fat envelope.

Line a large bamboo steamer with the extra lettuce leaves. Put the parcels in the steamer and cover with the lid. Place over a wok of simmering water and steam for 10–12 minutes, or until firm.

Serve hot or cold, sprinkled with extra shredded chilli and lime leaves, as part of a Thai meal.

shanghai pork sticks

serves 4

dipping sauce

60 ml (2 fl oz/1/4 cup) **light soy sauce**

2¹/2 tablespoons **lemon juice**

1 **garlic clove**, minced

1/2 teaspoon minced **ginger**

1 teaspoon **soft brown sugar**

1/2 teaspoon **oyster sauce**

2–3 drops **chilli oil**

12 **lemon grass stems**

450 g (1 lb) lean **minced (ground) pork**

8 **water chestnuts**, roughly chopped

2 **garlic cloves**, chopped

1 **red Asian shallot**, roughly chopped

1 tablespoon **light soy sauce**

2 teaspoons **vegetable oil**

1/2 teaspoon **chilli oil**

1/4 teaspoon **sesame oil**

1 teaspoon **lemon juice**

1 teaspoon grated fresh **ginger**

1/4 teaspoon **soft brown sugar**

To make the dipping sauce, put the soy sauce, lemon juice, garlic, ginger, sugar, oyster sauce, chilli oil and 60 ml (2 fl oz/1/4 cup) of water in a small saucepan and bring to the boil over medium heat. Reduce the heat and simmer for 5 minutes, then remove from the heat and set aside to cool.

Trim the lemon grass stems to 12 cm (4¹/2 inch) lengths and discard the tough outer leaves. Put the pork, water chestnuts, garlic, shallot, soy sauce, oils, lemon juice, ginger and sugar in a small processor fitted with the metal blade. Add a large pinch of salt and whizz for 25–30 seconds, or until the mixture forms a paste. Divide the mixture into 12 portions and mould each into a sausage shape around the thinner end of a lemon grass stem.

Preheat the barbecue plate or chargrill pan to medium–high. Cook the pork sticks, turning often, for 7–8 minutes, or until crisp and browned. Serve hot, accompanied by the dipping sauce.

terrine of garden vegetables

serves 6–8

1 1/2 tablespoons **olive oil**

60 g (2 1/4 oz) **butter**

4 **leeks**, white part only, thinly sliced

2 **carrots**, cut into small chunks

2 large **parsnips**, cut into small chunks

2 **garlic cloves**

250 g (9 oz/1 2/3 cups) fresh or frozen **peas**

125 ml (4 fl oz/1/2 cup) **pouring cream**

3 **eggs**

grated **nutmeg**, to taste

freshly ground **white pepper**, to taste

1/4 teaspoon **ground ginger**

50 g (1 3/4 oz/1/2 cup) grated **parmesan cheese**

1 tablespoon chopped **mint**

shredded **spring onions (scallions)**, to serve

garlic butter sauce

100 g (3 1/2 oz) **butter**

4 **garlic cloves**, minced

125 ml (4 fl oz/1/2 cup) **pouring cream**

1 teaspoon **lemon juice**

Line the greased **loaf tin** with **baking paper**.

Cook the butter and garlic until the **butter** has melted and the **garlic** has started to brown.

Heat the olive oil and butter in a frying pan over medium–low heat. Add the leek and cook for 4–5 minutes, or until soft but not browned. Remove from the heat.

Cook the carrot in a small saucepan of boiling salted water for 12–15 minutes, or until tender, then drain. Cook the parsnip and garlic in a small saucepan of boiling salted water for 10–12 minutes, or until tender, then drain. Cook the peas in a small saucepan of boiling salted water for 6–8 minutes, or until tender, then drain.

Meanwhile, beat the cream and eggs together in a bowl. Add nutmeg, to taste, and season well with salt and freshly ground white pepper.

Preheat the oven to 170°C (325°F/Gas 3). Grease a 21 x 7 x 8 cm (8¼ x 2¾ x 3¼ inch) loaf (bar) tin and line with baking paper.

Put the carrot, ginger and half the leek in a small processor fitted with the metal blade. Whizz for 45–60 seconds, or until puréed. Add one-third of the cream mixture and whizz until combined. Spoon into the prepared tin and level the surface. Sprinkle the top with 1 tablespoon of the parmesan.

Add the parsnip and garlic to the cleaned processor bowl and whizz for 30 seconds, or until puréed. Add half the remaining cream mixture and all but 1 tablespoon of the parmesan. Whizz until combined. Spoon gently over the carrot mixture and level the surface. Sprinkle the top with the remaining parmesan.

Add the peas, mint and remaining leek to the cleaned processor bowl and whizz for 45 seconds, or until puréed. Add the remaining cream mixture and whizz until combined. Spoon gently over the parsnip mixture and level the surface. Cover with a greased sheet of baking paper, then cover the tin with foil and seal the edges. Put the loaf tin in a roasting tin and pour in boiling water to a depth of 4 cm (1½ inches). Bake for 1½–1¾ hours, or until set. Remove from the oven and set aside to rest for 10 minutes.

Meanwhile, to make the garlic butter sauce, cook the butter and garlic in a small saucepan over medium heat for 1 minute, or until the butter has melted and turned golden and the garlic has started to brown. Strain, discard the solids and return the mixture to a clean saucepan. Add the cream and lemon juice and bring to the boil. Reduce the heat and simmer for 4–5 minutes, or until thickened. Season with salt.

Gently invert the terrine onto a serving plate and peel off the baking paper. Garnish with the shredded spring onion and serve warm with the garlic butter sauce.

asparagus mousse with lemon sauce

serves 4

150 g (5¹/2 oz) **asparagus**

1 **leek**, white part only

20 g (³/4 oz) **butter**

200 ml (7 fl oz) **pouring cream**

2 tablespoons chopped **mint**

1 tablespoon chopped **parsley**

4 **eggs**, lightly beaten

lemon sauce

50 g (1³/4 oz) **butter**

1 tablespoon **lemon juice**

Preheat the oven to 160°C (315°F/Gas 2–3). Grease 4 x 150 ml (5 fl oz) dariole moulds or ramekins.

Trim the asparagus and blanch in boiling water for 1 minute. Refresh in iced water, then drain and cut into 5 cm (2 inch) lengths. Slice the leek in half lengthways and thinly slice it.

Melt the butter in a large frying pan over low heat. Add the leek and cook for 10 minutes, then add the asparagus and cook for 5 minutes. Increase the heat to medium and add half the cream. Simmer for 1 minute, or until the cream has reduced and thickened a little.

Transfer to a blender and whizz for 15–20 seconds, or until smooth. Add the mint, parsley and remaining cream and whizz for 5–6 seconds. Add the eggs and whizz in short bursts until combined.

Pour the mixture into the prepared moulds or ramekins and place in a roasting tin. Pour enough hot water into the tin to come halfway up the sides of the moulds. Bake for 40–45 minutes, or until the mousse is set and brown on top. Set aside for 5 minutes.

Meanwhile, to make the lemon sauce, melt the butter in a small saucepan over medium–low heat until foaming. Strain through a fine sieve into a second small saucepan and add the lemon juice. Season, to taste.

Invert the mousse onto serving plates and drizzle with the lemon sauce.

feta, ricotta and prosciutto terrine

serves 10–12

200 g (7 oz) **prosciutto**, very thinly
  sliced

2 **red capsicums (peppers)**

350 g (12 oz/1¹/3 cups) **ricotta cheese**

200 g (7 oz) **feta cheese**

1¹/2 tablespoons **lemon juice**

2 tablespoons chopped **basil**

1¹/2 teaspoons **powdered gelatine**

80 ml (2¹/2 fl oz/¹/3 cup) **thick**
  (double/heavy) cream

1 handful **basil**

rocket (arugula) leaves, to serve

Grease an 18 x 9 x 6 cm (7 x 3¹/2 x 2¹/2 inch) loaf (bar) tin and line the tin with plastic wrap, pressing it into the edges. Reserve 8 prosciutto slices and use the remainder to line the tin, allowing the ends to overhang the edges of the tin.

Preheat the grill (broiler) to high. Arrange the whole capsicums on a wire rack and grill (broil) for 6–8 minutes on each side, or until evenly blackened. Cool in a plastic bag, then peel and discard the skin. Remove the seeds and cut the flesh into thick strips.

Put the ricotta, feta, lemon juice and chopped basil in a small processor fitted with the plastic blade. Whizz for 10–12 seconds, or until combined. Season well with salt and freshly ground black pepper and whizz for 8 seconds, or until semi-smooth. Transfer to a bowl. Finely chop half of the reserved prosciutto and stir through the cheese mixture.

Put the gelatine in a small bowl with 1 tablespoon of cold water and stir until the gelatine has dissolved. Pour the cream into a small saucepan, add the gelatine mixture and heat gently, stirring, for 1 minute. Stir in a little of the ricotta mixture, then stir this back into the rest of the ricotta mixture.

Spread one-third of the ricotta mixture into the prepared tin and top with half the capsicum strips. Add half the basil leaves in a layer on top of the capsicum. Cover with another third of the ricotta mixture, a final layer of capsicum and the remaining basil. Spread the remaining ricotta mixture over the top. Fold over the ends of the prosciutto and cover with the remaining reserved prosciutto slices. Wrap the tin in plastic wrap and chill overnight.

Invert the terrine onto a board and remove the plastic wrap. Use a sharp knife to cut the terrine into slices. Serve with the rocket leaves.

thai fried prawn balls
with spicy cucumber salad

serves 4

salad

2 **Lebanese (short) cucumbers**

2 tablespoons chopped **roasted peanuts**

1 small handful **coriander (cilantro) leaves**, roughly chopped

1 tablespoon **rice vinegar**

1/2 **red chilli**, shredded

1 small handful **Thai basil**, torn if large

600 g (1 lb 5 oz) **raw prawns (shrimp)**, peeled and deveined

1 small handful **coriander (cilantro) leaves**

2 **garlic cloves**, chopped

2 **egg whites**

1/2 teaspoon **salt**

1/2 teaspoon **ground white pepper**

2–4 drops **chilli oil**, to taste

80 ml (21/2 fl oz/1/3 cup) **peanut oil**

sweet chilli sauce, to serve

Toss the **cucumber**, peanuts, coriander, vinegar, **chilli** and Thai basil to make **the salad**.

Put the **prawns**, coriander leaves, **garlic**, egg whites, salt, pepper and **chilli oil** in a processor.

To make the salad, thinly peel the cucumbers and halve lengthways. Scrape out the seeds with a teaspoon and cut into 5 mm (1/4 inch) slices. Put in a bowl and toss with the peanuts, coriander, vinegar, chilli and Thai basil.

Put the prawns, coriander leaves, garlic, egg whites, salt, pepper and chilli oil, to taste, in a small processor fitted with the metal blade. Whizz for 40 seconds, or until the mixture forms a paste.

Heat the peanut oil in a wok over medium–high heat. Using a metal spoon dipped in cold water, spoon heaped tablespoons of the prawn mixture into the oil. Fry, turning, for 3–4 minutes, or until golden brown. Drain on paper towels.

Serve the prawn balls immediately, accompanied by the cucumber salad and a small bowl of sweet chilli sauce. Serve as part of a Thai meal.

chicken, pancetta and pine nut terrines

serves 10

125 g (4¹/2 oz) piece **pancetta**, diced

60 g (2¹/4 oz) **unsalted butter**, softened

1 **onion**, finely chopped

300 g (10¹/2 oz) boneless, skinless **chicken breasts**, roughly chopped

2 tablespoons **brandy**

80 ml (2¹/2 fl oz/¹/3 cup) **thick (double/heavy) cream**

25 g (1 oz/¹/3 cup) fresh **breadcrumbs**

2 tablespoons chopped **tarragon**

40 g (1¹/2 oz/¹/4 cup) **toasted pine nuts**

slices of **baguette**, to serve

capers, to serve

extra **tarragon sprigs**, to serve

Grease 10 small ramekins.

Heat a frying pan over high heat for 2 minutes, or until hot, add the pancetta and stir-fry for 3–4 minutes, or until the pancetta is lightly browned and the fat has rendered. Add half the butter and reduce the heat to low. Add the onion and fry gently for 5 minutes, or until softened. Add the chicken and cook for 5 minutes. Stir in the brandy, cover and cook for 3 minutes, or until the chicken is cooked through.

Transfer the mixture to a small processor fitted with the metal blade. Add the remaining butter, the cream, breadcrumbs, tarragon and pine nuts and whizz for 8 seconds, or until roughly chopped. Spoon the mixture into the prepared ramekins, pressing down firmly and smoothing the surface. Refrigerate for 4 hours, or until firm to the touch.

Invert the terrines onto serving plates and serve with baguette slices, garnished with capers and tarragon.

tip The terrine mixture can also be set in a loaf (bar) tin and served in slices.

zucchini timbales with lime buttermilk cream

serves 6

lime buttermilk cream
150 ml (5 fl oz) **pouring cream**

2¹/2 tablespoons **buttermilk**

1 teaspoon finely grated **lime zest**

white pepper, to taste

40 g (1¹/2 oz) **butter**

2 **leeks**, white part only, thinly sliced

350 g (12 oz) **zucchini (courgettes)**, trimmed

1 small handful **mint**

1 small handful **basil**

3 **eggs**

150 ml (5 fl oz) **pouring cream**

2¹/2 tablespoons **buttermilk**

extra **basil**, to serve

To make the lime buttermilk cream, combine the cream and buttermilk in a glass bowl and set aside at room temperature for 6 hours or overnight, or until the mixture has the consistency of custard. Add the lime zest and season with salt and white pepper, to taste.

Preheat the oven to 170°C (325°F/Gas 3). Grease six 200 ml (7 fl oz) timbale or dariole moulds.

Melt the butter in a small frying pan over low heat and cook the leek for 5 minutes, or until soft.

Add the zucchini to a saucepan of boiling salted water and simmer over medium heat for 8–10 minutes, or until tender. Drain and cut the zucchini into chunks.

Transfer the zucchini to a processor fitted with the metal blade and add the leek, mint and basil. Whizz for 20–25 seconds, or until finely chopped. Add the eggs, cream and buttermilk and whizz until just combined. Season with salt and freshly ground black pepper.

Pour the zucchini mixture into the prepared moulds and cover each with a circle of baking paper. Put in a large roasting tin and pour in boiling water to a depth of 4 cm (1½ inches). Bake for 30–35 minutes, or until firm. Set aside to cool for 5 minutes.

Invert the timbales onto serving plates and serve warm, garnished with extra basil leaves and accompanied by the lime buttermilk cream.

Fry the sliced leek in
the melted **butter** until
the leek is soft.

Add the **eggs**, cream and
buttermilk to the zucchini and
leek mixture.

331

desserts

sweet surrender

The whole spectrum of decadent desserts is at your fingertips — whizz up summery sorbets, creamy mousses, rich cheesecakes and melt-in-the-mouth tarts and pastries. With the irresistible flavours of beautiful berries and other seasonal fruits, creamy custards and rich chocolate, be prepared for calls of 'Bravo!' and 'Encore!' as you serve up your spectacular creations. Take your bow, take your spoon and relax as you contemplate what's more rewarding — bathing in the glow of the faces of your satisfied diners, or indulging in the fruits of your labour.

white chocolate mousse

serves 6

150 g (51/2 oz/1 cup) roughly chopped **white chocolate**

50 g (13/4 oz) **unsalted butter**

1 teaspoon **natural vanilla extract**

3 **eggs**, separated

1 **egg white**

2 tablespoons **caster (superfine) sugar**

125 ml (4 fl oz/1/2 cup) **thickened (whipping) cream**, whipped

white chocolate shavings, to serve

Put the chocolate in a small processor fitted with the metal blade and whizz for 15 seconds, or until finely chopped. Melt the butter and vanilla extract in a small saucepan over low heat. Add to the processor containing the chocolate and whizz for 8–10 seconds, or until the chocolate has melted and the mixture is smooth. With the motor running, add the egg yolks one at a time and whizz until just combined. Transfer to a large bowl.

Put the four egg whites in a large processor fitted with the whisk attachment and whisk until soft peaks form. With the motor running, gradually add the caster sugar and whisk until stiff peaks form. (This step can also be done using electric beaters.) Fold a spoonful of the egg whites into the chocolate mixture, then gently fold in the remaining egg whites.

Very carefully fold the whipped cream through the chocolate mixture until it is well combined. Divide the mixture among six bowls, cover with plastic wrap and refrigerate overnight.

Serve the mousse topped with the white chocolate shavings.

coffee granita with crushed coffee beans

serves 8–10

300 g (10 1/2 oz/1 1/3 cups) **sugar**

1 litre (35 fl oz/4 cups) freshly made **espresso coffee**

55 g (2 oz/1/3 cup) **chocolate-coated coffee beans**

Stir the sugar into the hot coffee until the sugar has dissolved. Set aside to cool, then transfer to a deep plastic container.

Freeze the mixture for 1–2 hours, or until ice crystals have formed around the edges. Using an immersion blender or blender, whizz for 15–20 seconds to break up the ice crystals. Return to the freezer and repeat this method every 30 minutes or so until the mixture reaches a coarse snowy texture.

Put the chocolate-coated coffee beans in a mini processor or coffee grinder and whizz briefly until roughly ground.

Serve the granita in chilled glasses topped with a sprinkling of the beans.

crustless redcurrant cheesecake

serves 6–8

150 g (5¹/2 oz/1¹/4 cups) **toasted slivered almonds**

750 g (1 lb 10 oz) **neufchatel cheese** (see tips, page 342)

2 tablespoons **plain (all-purpose) flour**

300 g (10¹/2 oz/1¹/3 cups) **caster (superfine) sugar**

2 teaspoons **natural vanilla extract**

1¹/2 teaspoons finely grated **lemon zest**

4 **eggs**

125 g (4¹/2 oz/1 cup) **redcurrants** (see tips, page 342), plus extra to serve

2 teaspoons **crème de cassis** or **cherry brandy**

1 tablespoon **icing (confectioners') sugar**

topping

300 g (10¹/2 oz/1¹/4 cups) **sour cream**

2 tablespoons **caster (superfine) sugar**

1 teaspoon **natural vanilla extract**

Preheat the oven to 170°C (325°F/Gas 3). Grease a 22 cm (8½ inch) spring-form cake tin. Put the almonds in a large processor fitted with the metal blade and whizz in 2-second bursts for 12 seconds, or until they resemble fine breadcrumbs. Do not grind the almonds to a powder. Transfer the almonds to the prepared tin and roll the tin around to coat with the almonds. Spread the excess almonds over the base of the tin.

Put the neufchatel cheese, flour, caster sugar, vanilla and lemon zest in the cleaned processor and whizz for 12–15 seconds, or until smooth. Add the eggs and whizz for 10 seconds, or until well combined, scraping down the side of the bowl as needed. Transfer the mixture to a bowl.

Without cleaning the processor bowl, add the redcurrants, crème de cassis or cherry brandy and icing sugar and whizz for 10–12 seconds, or until smooth. Add 250 ml (9 fl oz/1 cup) of the cheese mixture and briefly whizz to combine.

Gently pour the remaining cheese mixture into the tin, being careful not to disturb the almond crumbs. Bake for 20 minutes. Gently spoon the redcurrant mixture over the surface and bake for a further 30 minutes, or until the surface is just set. Remove from the oven and set aside to cool for 15 minutes.

To make the topping, mix the sour cream, sugar and vanilla in a small bowl until smooth. Spread over the cheesecake and return to the oven for 10 minutes. Set aside to cool in the tin, then turn out and chill before serving. Serve topped with extra redcurrants.

tips Neufchatel cheese is a fresh cream cheese, available from delicatessens. Use fresh or frozen redcurrants or blackcurrants. If frozen, thaw and drain them before use.

Put the chopped almonds in the tin and **roll the tin** around to coat the base and side with the **almonds**.

Add the **redcurrants**, liqueur and icing sugar to the processor and **whizz** until smooth.

mango and lime gelato

serves 4–6

235 g (8¹/2 oz/1 cup) **caster (superfine) sugar**

2 large ripe **mangoes**, chopped (see tip)

60 ml (2 fl oz/¹/4 cup) **lime juice**

1 teaspoon grated **lime zest**

Put the sugar and 500 ml (17 fl oz/2 cups) of water in a small saucepan and stir over medium–low heat until the sugar has dissolved. Bring to the boil, then reduce the heat and simmer for 10 minutes. Remove from the heat and cool almost to room temperature.

Put the mango in a blender or small processor fitted with the metal blade and whizz for 20 seconds, or until puréed. Add the cooled sugar syrup and lime juice and whizz for 30 seconds, or until thoroughly blended. Pour into a shallow metal tin and stir in the lime zest.

Freeze the mixture for 1¹/2 hours, or until almost frozen. Whizz again in the blender or processor to break up the ice crystals, then return to the freezer in the tin until completely frozen.

Use a metal spoon to scoop the gelato into glasses or bowls.

tip You will need 750 g (1 lb 10 oz/3¹/2 cups) of mango flesh.

raspberry semifreddo

serves 6–8

235 g (8½ oz/2 cups) **raspberries** (see tips), plus extra for serving

110 g (3¾ oz/1 cup) **icing (confectioners') sugar**

1½ tablespoons **lime juice**

200 g (7 oz/¾ cup) **Greek-style yoghurt**

300 ml (10½ fl oz) **thickened (whipping) cream**

wafers, to serve

Put the raspberries, sugar, lime juice and yoghurt in a blender and whizz for 20–25 seconds, or until smooth.

Whisk the cream in a bowl until soft peaks form. Gently fold the raspberry mixture into the cream. Pour into a shallow metal tin, cover with plastic wrap or foil and freeze for 1–1½ hours, or until the edges are frozen.

Line a 1 litre (35 fl oz/4 cup) loaf (bar) tin with plastic wrap so that it overhangs the edges. Return the raspberry mixture to the blender and whizz for 6–10 seconds, or until smooth. Transfer to the prepared tin and smooth the top. Fold the plastic wrap over the top and freeze for at least 4 hours, or until set.

Remove the tin from the freezer and leave at room temperature for 2–3 minutes. Lift the semifreddo from the tin using the plastic wrap and cut into slices. Sandwich between 2 wafers that have been trimmed to fit. Serve with extra raspberries.

tips Use fresh raspberries or thawed frozen raspberries.

almond fudge cheesecake with ginger crust

serves 6–8

crust

185 g (6 1/2 oz) **ginger nut biscuits (ginger snaps)**, roughly broken

60 g (2 1/4 oz) **butter**, melted

filling

750 g (1 lb 10 oz/3 cups) **cream cheese**, softened

250 g (9 oz/1 cup) **raw or golden caster (superfine) sugar**

3 **eggs**

1/2 teaspoon **almond extract**

2 teaspoons **natural vanilla extract**

topping

185 g (6 1/2 oz/1 cup) **dark chocolate chips**

60 g (2 1/4 oz) **butter**

60 g (2 1/4 oz/2/3 cup) **toasted flaked almonds**

Preheat the oven to 180°C (350°F/Gas 4). Grease a 22 cm (8½ inch) spring-form cake tin and line the base with baking paper.

To make the crust, put the biscuits in a large processor fitted with the metal blade. Whizz for 20–25 seconds, or until the biscuits form fine crumbs. Add the melted butter and whizz for 8–10 seconds, or until combined. Press the crust firmly over the base of the prepared tin. Chill until firm.

To make the filling, wipe out the processor bowl and add the cream cheese. Whizz for 20–25 seconds, or until smooth, scraping down the side of the bowl as needed. Add the sugar, eggs, almond extract and vanilla and whizz in 5-second bursts for 15–20 seconds, or until well blended.

Pour the filling into the prepared tin. Bake for 45 minutes, or until set. Turn off the oven, prop the door slightly ajar and leave to cool for 30 minutes, then remove from the oven and cool completely.

To make the topping, put the chocolate and butter in a small heatproof bowl. Place over a saucepan of simmering water, ensuring that the water doesn't touch the bottom of the bowl. Heat, stirring occasionally, until melted and smooth. Stir in the almonds.

Spread the topping over the top of the cheesecake and allow to set before serving.

Press the **crust** mixture firmly over the **base of the tin**.

Heat the chocolate and butter over a saucepan of **simmering water** until melted and smooth.

351

chocolate hazelnut cake

serves 6–8

200 g (7 oz/1¹/2 cups) **roasted skinned hazelnut**

200 g (7 oz/1¹/3 cups) chopped good-quality **dark chocolate**

2 teaspoons **espresso instant coffee granules**

100 g (3¹/2 oz/³/4 cup) **cornflour (cornstarch)**

200 g (7 oz) **unsalted butter**, softened

185 g (6¹/2 oz/³/4 cup) **raw or golden caster (superfine) sugar**

4 **eggs**, separated

2 teaspoons **hazelnut liqueur** or **coffee liqueur**

icing (confectioners') sugar, to serve

cocoa flakes, optional, to serve

crème fraîche or **vanilla ice cream**, to serve

Preheat the oven to 170°C (325°F/Gas 3) and grease a 20 cm (8 inch) spring-form cake tin.

Put the hazelnuts and chocolate in a small processor fitted with the metal blade and whizz in 5-second bursts until finely chopped. Add the coffee granules and cornflour and whizz briefly to combine. Transfer to a small bowl and set aside.

Change the blade on the processor to the plastic blade. Add the butter and sugar and whizz in 3-second bursts until pale. Add one-quarter of the chocolate mixture, whizz in short bursts to combine, then add 1 egg yolk and whizz in short bursts to mix through. Continue in this way until all the chocolate mixture and egg yolks have been added. Add the liqueur and whizz in short bursts to combine. Transfer to a bowl.

Whisk the egg whites until soft peaks form. Using a metal spoon, fold a large scoop of egg whites into the chocolate mixture. Gently fold in the remaining egg whites. Spoon into the prepared tin, level the surface and bake for 30 minutes. Cover loosely with foil and bake for a further 30–35 minutes, or until a skewer inserted in the centre of the cake comes out clean. The surface of the cake will probably crack.

Serve the cake warm or at room temperature. Dust the surface with icing sugar and sprinkle with the cocoa flakes, if using. Cut the cake into slices; the texture will be quite moist. Serve with a scoop of crème fraîche or soft vanilla ice cream.

banana soy milk pancakes with honeycomb butter

serves 4

honeycomb butter

60 g (2¼ oz) **butter**, softened

1 tablespoon **honey**

50 g crushed **honeycomb**

pancakes

2 **bananas**

325–375 ml (11–13 fl oz) **vanilla soy milk**

2 **eggs**

1 tablespoon **caster (superfine) sugar**

30 g (1 oz) **butter**, melted

1 teaspoon **natural vanilla extract**

185 g (6½ oz/1½ cups) **self-raising flour**

½ teaspoon **bicarbonate of soda (baking soda)**

icing (confectioners') sugar, to serve

ice cream, to serve

Beat the softened butter and **honey** together.

Cook each pancake on the first side until **bubbles appear** on the surface.

To make the honeycomb butter, beat the butter and honey together, then fold through the crushed honeycomb.

To make the pancakes, cut one of the bananas into pieces and put in a blender. Add three-quarters of the soy milk, the eggs, sugar, melted butter and vanilla. Whizz for 10–15 seconds, or until the batter is smooth. Add the remaining soy milk a little at a time.

Add the flour and bicarbonate of soda and whizz in short bursts for 30 seconds, or until well combined and smooth. Pour the batter into a pitcher. Thinly slice the remaining banana and stir it into the batter.

Heat a large non-stick frying pan over medium heat and lightly grease with melted butter. Pour 60 ml (2 fl oz/1/4 cup) of the batter into the pan and cook for 2 minutes, or until bubbles appear on the surface. Turn and cook for 2 minutes or until cooked and golden. Transfer the pancake to a wire rack and cover with a tea towel (dish towel) to keep warm while you cook the remaining pancakes.

Serve the pancakes dusted with icing sugar and topped with a small scoop of ice cream and the honeycomb butter.

passionfruit cream with snap biscuits

serves 6–8

snap biscuits

100 g (3¹/2 oz/²/3 cup) **blanched almonds**

115 g (4 oz/¹/2 cup) **caster (superfine) sugar**

60 g (2¹/4 oz) **unsalted butter**, softened

1 tablespoon **plain (all-purpose) flour**

1 **egg white**

8 **passionfruit**

125 g (4¹/2 oz/1 cup) **raspberries**

250 g (9 oz/1 cup) **ricotta cheese**

50 g (1³/4 oz/¹/2 cup) **icing (confectioners') sugar**, sifted, plus extra for dusting

¹/2 teaspoon **natural vanilla extract**

150 ml (5 fl oz) **thickened (whipping) cream**, whipped

Drop teaspoons of the biscuit mixture onto the baking sheet and **flatten with** the back of a spoon.

Strain the **passionfruit** through a fine sieve and **discard** the pulp.

To make the snap biscuits, preheat the oven to 180°C (350°F/Gas 4). Line two baking sheets with baking paper.

Put the almonds and half the caster sugar in a small processor fitted with the metal blade and whizz for 1 minute, or until a fine powder forms. Add the remaining sugar, the butter, flour and egg white and whizz until just combined.

Drop rounded teaspoons of mixture 5 cm (2 inches) apart onto one of the prepared baking sheets and flatten them with the back of a spoon. Bake for 7–8 minutes, or until golden. Remove from the oven and slide the paper with the biscuits onto a flat surface to cool. Repeat with the remaining mixture.

Halve six of the passionfruit and strain the juice through a fine sieve into a bowl. Discard the pulp. Halve the remaining passionfruit, scoop the pulp into a bowl and gently stir in the raspberries, reserving a few raspberries for garnishing. Cover and chill until needed.

Put the ricotta, icing sugar, vanilla and strained passionfruit juice into the clean processor fitted with the plastic blade. Whizz for 30 seconds, then scrape down the side of the bowl. Repeat until the mixture is smooth. Transfer to a large bowl. Using a metal spoon, carefully fold the whipped cream through the ricotta mixture until well combined. Cover and refrigerate until needed.

To serve, gently fold the raspberry mixture through the passionfruit cream. Put one of the snap biscuits on each plate, spoon on the passionfruit cream, then top with another biscuit. Dust with icing sugar and garnish with the reserved raspberries. Serve immediately.

tip Any leftover biscuits can be kept in an airtight container for 3–4 days.

peach yoghurt mousse

serves 4

125 g (4^1/2 oz/1 cup) **dried peaches**

250 ml (9 fl oz/1 cup) **peach nectar**

2 teaspoons **powdered gelatine**

200 g (7 oz/^{3}/4 cup) **plain yoghurt**

2–3 teaspoons **honey**, to taste

3 **egg whites**

2 tablespoons **toasted flaked almonds**, to serve

Put the peaches and peach nectar in a small saucepan. Cook over low heat, stirring often, for 10 minutes, or until the peaches are soft and pulpy. Set aside to cool for 10 minutes.

Put 2 tablespoons of hot water in a small bowl and sprinkle the gelatine over the top. Whisk with a fork for 1 minute, or until the gelatine has dissolved.

Put the peach mixture, gelatine mixture and yoghurt in a blender or small processor fitted with the metal blade. Whizz for 20–30 seconds, or until smooth. Add the honey, to taste, and whizz to combine.

Whisk the egg whites until firm peaks form. Pour the peach mixture into the egg whites and gently fold through using a metal spoon.

Spoon the mousse into 4 x 250 ml (9 fl oz/1 cup) parfait glasses and smooth the surface. Cover and refrigerate for at least 1 hour, or until firm. Serve sprinkled with the almonds.

blood orange and champagne sorbet

serves 6–8

115 g (4 oz/1/2 cup) **caster (superfine) sugar**

500 ml (17 fl oz/2 cups) **blood orange juice** (see tip)

150 ml (5 fl oz) **Champagne**

2 tablespoons **Campari**

Put the sugar and 250 ml (9 fl oz/1 cup) of water in a heavy-based saucepan. Stir constantly over medium–low heat until the sugar has dissolved, then stop stirring. Bring to the boil, then reduce the heat and simmer for 5 minutes. Cool.

Put the sugar syrup, blood orange juice, Champagne and Campari in a blender or processor fitted with the plastic blade. Whizz for 15–20 seconds, or until thoroughly combined. Pour into ice cube trays and freeze for 2 hours, or until firm.

Turn the frozen mixture out of the trays and return to the blender or processor. Whizz in 5-second bursts until the mixture forms a coarse, icy purée. Transfer to a plastic container and return to the freezer for 1 hour.

Remove the sorbet from the freezer and break it up with a fork. Work quickly, as it will melt quickly. Spoon the sorbet into bowls or glasses and serve immediately.

tip You will need about six oranges to make 500 ml (17 fl oz/2 cups) of juice. If blood oranges are not in season, substitute other oranges.

strawberry and rhubarb tart

serves 6–8

pastry

100 g (3 1/2 oz) **unsalted butter**

55 g (2 oz/1/4 cup) **caster (superfine) sugar**

200 g (7 oz/1 2/3 cups) **plain (all-purpose) flour**

1 **egg**, lightly beaten

filling

100 ml (3 1/2 fl oz) **milk**

125 ml (4 fl oz/1/2 cup) **pouring cream**

1 teaspoon **natural vanilla extract**

2 x 5 cm (3/4 x 2 inch) piece **lemon zest**, white pith removed

6 **egg yolks**

55 g (2 oz/1/4 cup) **caster (superfine) sugar**

2 teaspoons **plain (all-purpose) flour**

300 g (10 1/2 oz) **rhubarb**, cut into 2 cm (3/4 inch) lengths

250 g (9 oz/1 2/3 cups) small **strawberries**, hulled

Add 1 teaspoon of cold water at a time and **whizz until** the dough clumps together.

Prick **the base** of the pastry **with a fork** before baking.

To make the pastry, put the butter and sugar in a small processor fitted with the metal blade. Whizz for 30 seconds, or until combined. Add the flour and a pinch of salt and whizz until just combined. Add the egg and whizz for 10 seconds. With the motor running, add 1 teaspoon of cold water at a time until the dough clumps together. Turn out onto a floured surface and knead until smooth. Form into a ball, flatten slightly, cover with plastic wrap and chill for 30 minutes.

Preheat the oven to 200°C (400°F/Gas 6). Grease a 30 cm (12 inch) loose-based tart tin. Roll out the pastry between two sheets of baking paper until it is 4 mm (1/8 inch) thick and use it to line the prepared tin. Trim the excess pastry, leaving 5 mm (1/4 inch) above the tin. Prick the base with a fork, line with a piece of crumpled baking paper and pour in some baking beads or uncooked rice. Bake for 15 minutes, then remove the paper and beads and return to the oven for another 8 minutes, or until lightly golden.

Reduce the oven to 180°C (350°F/Gas 4). Place a baking tray on the centre rack.

To make the filling, put the milk, cream, vanilla and lemon zest in a heavy-based saucepan. Gently heat over low heat for 8 minutes, or until just below boiling point. Remove and set aside to infuse for 10 minutes. Discard the lemon zest.

Put the egg yolks, sugar and flour in the cleaned processor. With the motor running, gradually add the infused milk and whizz until the custard is smooth. Pour into the prepared pastry case and arrange the rhubarb and strawberries over the top.

Put the tart on the baking tray in the oven and bake for 35–40 minutes, or until set. Check the tart after 20 minutes and place a sheet of foil over the top if it is browning too quickly. Serve warm or at room temperature.

mascarpone tart with blueberries

serves 4–6

pastry

185 g (6 1/2 oz/1 1/2 cups)
   plain (all-purpose) flour

2 tablespoons **caster (superfine) sugar**

1 teaspoon finely grated **lemon zest**

90 g (3 1/4 oz/1/3 cup) **sour cream**

2–3 tablespoons **light olive oil**

250 g (9 oz/1 1/4 cups) **mascarpone cheese**

60 g (2 1/4 oz/1/4 cup) **sour cream**

165 g (5 3/4 oz/3/4 cup) **raw or golden caster (superfine) sugar**

1/2 teaspoon finely grated **lemon zest**

1 teaspoon **natural vanilla extract**

2 tablespoons **cornflour (cornstarch)**

4 **egg yolks**

100 g (3 1/2 oz/2/3 cup) **blueberries**

icing (confectioners') sugar, to serve

To make the pastry, put the flour, sugar, lemon zest, sour cream and a large pinch of salt in a small processor fitted with the plastic blade. Whizz for 8–10 seconds, or until combined. With the motor running, gradually add the olive oil, stopping once the mixture resembles wet breadcrumbs. Remove from the processor and knead briefly to form a smooth ball. Cover with plastic wrap and chill for 30 minutes.

Preheat the oven to 190°C (375°F/Gas 5). Grease an 18 cm (7 inch) loose-based tart tin. Roll out the pastry between two sheets of baking paper to a circle large enough to fit the prepared tin. Use the pastry to line the tin, then trim the edges. Line the pastry with a piece of crumpled baking paper and pour in some baking beads or uncooked rice. Bake for 12 minutes, then remove the paper and beads and return to the oven for another 8 minutes, or until golden. Set aside to cool for 10 minutes.

Meanwhile, put the mascarpone, sour cream and sugar in the cleaned processor. Whizz for 15–20 seconds, or until smooth. Add the lemon zest, vanilla, cornflour and egg yolks and whizz for 12–15 seconds, or until combined.

Transfer the mixture to a metal bowl over a saucepan of simmering water. Cook, stirring often, for 30 minutes, or until the mixture is thickened and holds its shape. Spoon into the pastry case and level the surface. Sprinkle the blueberries over the surface, pressing them in gently. Set aside to cool completely. Serve dusted with icing sugar.

sweet pumpkin pie

serves 8–10

pastry

185 g (6¹/2 oz/1¹/2 cups)
  plain (all-purpose) flour

125 g (4¹/2 oz) unsalted butter, chilled
  and cubed

3 teaspoons sugar

1 teaspoon finely grated orange zest

1 egg yolk

700 g (1 lb 9 oz) jap (kent) pumpkin
  (squash), peeled, seeded and cubed

80 ml (2¹/2 fl oz/¹/3 cup) pouring cream

1 teaspoon ground cinnamon

1/2 teaspoon ground ginger

1/2 teaspoon mixed (pumpkin pie) spice

1–2 tablespoons maple syrup

2 tablespoons soft brown sugar

2 eggs

mixed (pumpkin pie) spice, to serve

To make the pastry, put the flour, butter, sugar and orange zest in a small processor fitted with the plastic blade. Whizz in 5-second bursts until the mixture resembles breadcrumbs. Add the egg yolk and 2 tablespoons of cold water and process until the dough comes together into a ball. Add more water if needed, 1 teaspoon at a time. Remove from the processor, shape into a disc and cover with plastic wrap. Chill for 30 minutes.

Put the pumpkin in a saucepan and cover with water. Bring to the boil, then simmer for 15–20 minutes, or until tender. Drain thoroughly and set aside to cool. You will need 400 g (14 oz/2 cups) of cooked pumpkin. Put the pumpkin in the cleaned processor or a blender and add the cream, cinnamon, ginger, mixed spice, maple syrup, sugar and eggs. Whizz for 30–40 seconds, or until finely puréed.

Preheat the oven to 200°C (400°F/Gas 6). Grease a 23 cm (9 inch) loose-based flan tin. Roll out the pastry between two sheets of baking paper to a circle large enough to fit the prepared tin. Use the pastry to line the tin. Line the pastry with a piece of crumpled baking paper and pour in some baking beads or uncooked rice. Bake for 10 minutes, then remove the paper and beads and return to the oven for another 10 minutes, or until golden. Set aside to cool for 5 minutes. Reduce the oven to 180°C (350°F/Gas 4) and place a baking tray on the centre rack.

Pour the filling into the pastry shell. Put the pie on the baking tray in the oven and bake for 40–45 minutes, or until set. Serve warm or at room temperature, with thick (double/heavy) cream, sprinkled with mixed spice.

chestnut, ginger and pistachio loaf

serves 10–12

200 g (7 oz/11/3 cups) roughly chopped **dark chocolate**

110 g (33/4 oz) **butter**, chopped

875 g (1 lb 15 oz) **chestnut purée** (see tip, page 377)

40 g (11/2 oz/1/3 cup) **icing (confectioners') sugar**

60 ml (2 fl oz/1/4 cup) **mandarin liqueur** or **orange liqueur**

60 g (21/4 oz/1/3 cup) roughly chopped **preserved ginger**

70 g (21/2 oz/1/2 cup) **pistachio nuts**

70 g (21/2 oz/1/2 cup) **toasted slivered almonds**

extra **icing (confectioners') sugar**, to serve

Add the **chocolate** mixture to the puréed **chestnut mixture** and whizz until smooth.

Use the foil handles to **lift the loaf** out of the tin.

Put the chocolate and butter in a heatproof bowl and place over a saucepan of simmering water, ensuring that the water doesn't touch the bottom of the bowl. Heat, stirring occasionally, for 5–6 minutes, or until melted and smooth. Remove from the heat and set aside to cool for 10 minutes.

Put the chestnut purée, sugar and 2 tablespoons of the liqueur in a large processor fitted with the metal blade and whizz until smooth. Add the chocolate mixture and whizz until smooth. Add the ginger and half the pistachios and almonds. Whizz in 5-second bursts until the nuts are roughly chopped.

Line the base and two opposite sides of an 8 x 16 cm (3¼ x 6¼ inch) loaf (bar) tin with foil, allowing the foil to overhang the sides to help remove the loaf from the tin. Mix the remaining liqueur with 1 tablespoon of water and brush over the inside of the tin. Spoon the chestnut mixture into the tin, packing it down tightly to eliminate air pockets. Fold the foil overhang over the surface and cover with plastic wrap. Refrigerate for at least 3 hours, or until firm.

Using the foil handles, lift the loaf out of the tin. Peel off and discard the foil. Put the loaf on a serving plate, scatter the remaining nuts over the top and dust with icing sugar. Cut into slices to serve.

tip Tinned chestnut purée is acceptable to use, but you will get a better flavour from using the same weight of cooked peeled chestnuts and puréeing them yourself until very smooth.

apricot and coconut fool

serves 4

20 g (3/4 oz/1/3 cup) **shredded coconut**

300 ml (101/2 fl oz) **thickened (whipping) cream**

30 g (1 oz/1/4 cup) **icing (confectioners') sugar**

15 tinned **apricot halves**, drained

1 teaspoon **natural vanilla extract**

Preheat the grill (broiler) to medium–high. Spread the shredded coconut on a baking sheet. Place 12 cm (41/2 inches) below the heat and toast, stirring once or twice, for 3–4 minutes, or until just starting to brown.

Put the cream and 1 tablespoon of the sugar in a large processor fitted with the whisk attachment and whisk until medium peaks form. (This step can also be done using electric beaters.) Spoon into a large bowl.

Change the blade on the processor to the metal blade and add the apricot halves, vanilla and the remaining sugar. Whizz for 15 seconds, or until puréed.

Roughly fold the apricot mixture into the cream; do not completely combine, but leave ripples of the apricot running through the cream. Spoon into four glass bowls, sprinkle with the toasted coconut and serve.

tip This dish can be prepared in advance and refrigerated for several hours. Add the coconut just before serving.

palmiers with chocolate, hazelnut and orange filling

makes 45

20 g (3/4 oz/about 22) **roasted skinned hazelnuts**

2 teaspoons **caster (superfine) sugar**

1 1/2 tablespoons **dark chocolate chips**

large pinch of **ground cinnamon**

1 tablespoon **orange liqueur**

375 g (13 oz) block ready-made **puff pastry**, thawed

1 **egg**, lightly beaten

extra **caster (superfine) sugar**, for sprinkling

Preheat the oven to 200°C (400°F/Gas 6). Line two baking trays with baking paper.

Put the hazelnuts, sugar, chocolate chips and cinnamon in a small processor fitted with the metal blade. Whizz for 20 seconds, or until the mixture forms a fine paste. Add the liqueur and whizz to combine.

Roll the pastry out to a 20 x 33 cm (8 x 13 inch) rectangle, 5 mm (1/4 inch) thick. Spread the hazelnut mixture over the pastry. Tightly roll one long side of the pastry into the centre. Roll the opposite side in to meet in the middle. Cover with plastic wrap and chill for 30 minutes.

Brush the pastry all over with a little beaten egg and sprinkle with caster sugar. Using a sharp knife, cut the pastry into 5 mm (1/4 inch) slices. Place well apart on the prepared trays and brush very lightly with beaten egg. Bake for 10 minutes, then turn, brush lightly with egg and bake for 5–8 minutes, or until the palmiers are crisp and golden. Cool on wire racks.

tips Make sure you brush the pastry very lightly with egg. Egg in the pastry folds will bind them together and prevent even rising during baking. The palmiers will keep in an airtight container for 24 hours, but are at their best the day they are made.

mixed berry sundae with raspberry cream

serves 10

400 g (14 oz/1¾ cups) **sugar**

juice of 1 **lemon**

1 kg (2 lb 4 oz) **mixed summer berries**, including blueberries,
   loganberries, raspberries and strawberries

extra **fresh berries**, to serve

raspberry cream

250 g (9 oz/2 cups) fresh **raspberries**

50 g (1¾ oz/½ cup) **icing (confectioners') sugar**

125 ml (4 fl oz/½ cup) **thickened (whipping) cream**

Put 500 ml (17 fl oz/2 cups) of water in a saucepan and add the sugar. Heat gently over low heat until the sugar has dissolved. Bring to the boil, then reduce the heat and simmer for 5 minutes. Set aside to cool, then stir in the lemon juice.

Put the sugar syrup and mixed berries in a large processor fitted with the metal blade and whizz for 20 seconds, or until smooth. Press the purée through a sieve in batches and pour into a wide, deep plastic container.

Freeze the mixture for 1–2 hours, or until ice crystals have formed around the edges. Using an immersion blender or blender, whizz to break up the ice crystals. Return to the freezer and repeat this process for 4–5 hours until the berry mixture resembles soft snow.

To make the raspberry cream, whizz the raspberries and sugar in a small processor for 10 seconds, or until smooth. Press through a fine sieve. Lightly whip the cream until it just holds its shape. Fold the cream into the raspberry purée.

Serve the frozen sundae mixture in chilled glasses with a spoonful of raspberry cream and some fresh berries.

ruby plum sorbet

serves 6

150 ml (5 fl oz) freshly squeezed **orange juice**

grated **zest** of 1 **orange**

185 g (6¹/2 oz/³/4 cup) **caster (superfine) sugar**

820 g (1 lb 13 oz) tin whole **plums**, drained

¹/4 teaspoon **ground cinnamon**

Put the orange juice, orange zest, sugar and 150 ml (5 fl oz) of water in a saucepan. Stir over medium heat until the sugar has dissolved. Bring to the boil, then remove from the heat and set aside to cool.

Halve the plums and discard the seeds. Strain the orange syrup into a blender. Add the plums and cinnamon and whizz for 2–3 minutes, or until very smooth.

Pour the mixture into a 28 x 19 cm (11¹/4 x 7¹/2 inch) shallow metal tin, cover with plastic wrap or foil and freeze for 1–1¹/2 hours, or until the mixture starts to freeze around the edges. Return to the blender and whizz for 6–10 seconds, or until the mixture is smooth. Return to the tin, cover and freeze for 1 hour. Blend once more, then freeze until ready to serve.

pear and ginger filo parcels

serves 4

30 g (1 oz/1/4 cup) **flame raisins** or **other small seedless raisins**

1 tablespoon **cognac** or **pear eau-de-vie**

2 teaspoons **lemon juice**

3 **Bosc pears**

50 g (13/4 oz) **ginger nut biscuits (ginger snaps)**, roughly broken

40 g (11/2 oz/1/4 cup) **soft brown sugar**

1/2 teaspoon **mixed (pumpkin pie) spice**

2 tablespoons **cornflour (cornstarch)**

1 **egg yolk**

8 sheets **filo pastry**

canola oil spray

icing (confectioners') sugar, to serve

softened **vanilla ice cream**, to serve

Peel, quarter and core the pears, then add them to the bowl of **lemon juice**.

Whizz the ginger nut **biscuits**, sugar, mixed spice and cornflour until the **mixture forms** fine crumbs.

Preheat the oven to 190°C (375°F/Gas 5). Line a baking tray with baking paper.

Put the raisins and liqueur in a small bowl and set aside.

Put the lemon juice in a bowl. Peel, quarter and core the pears. Add them to the bowl and toss to coat with the lemon juice.

Put the ginger nut biscuits in a mini processor and add the sugar, mixed spice and cornflour. Whizz for 15 seconds, or until the mixture forms fine crumbs. Roughly chop half the pears and add to the processor. Add the egg yolk and whizz in 2-second bursts for 15–25 seconds, or until the pears are chopped medium–fine. The mixture will be quite thin.

Cut the remaining pears into 2 cm (3/4 inch) dice and return to their bowl. Add the raisin mixture and processed pear mixture and toss to combine.

Lay a sheet of filo on a work surface and spray with oil. Fold in half, one short side over the other and spray with oil. Top with another sheet of filo, fold that in half and spray with oil, giving four layers of pastry. Trim the pastry to an 18 cm (7 inch) square. Spoon one-quarter of the pear filling onto the centre. Starting at one corner, fold the filo over the filling to make a fat, square envelope. Ensure that the filling is well contained, and spray dry surfaces of the pastry as you fold. Spray the parcel all over with oil and place on the prepared tray, fold side up. Make three more parcels using the remaining pastry and filling.

Bake for 20–25 minutes, or until the parcels are crisp and golden. Serve hot, dusted with icing sugar and with a little softened vanilla ice cream spooned on top.

sweet ricotta tarts with walnut crust

serves 4

crust

200 g (7 oz/2 cups) **golden walnuts**

3 teaspoons **plain (all-purpose) flour**

2 tablespoons **raw or golden caster (superfine) sugar**

40 g (1 1/2 oz) **butter**, melted

filling

300 g (10 1/2 oz/1 1/4 cups) **ricotta cheese**

125 g (4 1/2 oz/1/2 cup) **raw or golden caster (superfine) sugar**

120 g (4 1/4 oz/1/2 cup) **crème fraîche** or **sour cream**

2 **eggs**

30 g (1 oz/1/4 cup) **plain (all-purpose) flour**

1 teaspoon **natural vanilla extract**

2 teaspoons **lemon juice**

Toss the **walnut** mixture around the insides of the tart tins to **coat** them.

Cover the top of each tart with strips of paper and **dust parallel lines** of the walnut mixture over the surface.

Preheat the oven to 170°C (325°F/Gas 3). Grease four 10.5 cm (4 inch) diameter, 2.5 cm (1 inch) deep loose-based tart tins and line the bases with baking paper.

To make the crust, put the walnuts, flour and sugar in a small processor fitted with the metal blade. Whizz in 5-second bursts for 25 seconds, or until fine (whizzing may bring out the oil in the walnuts, causing them to clump).

Remove 3 tablespoons of the walnut mixture. Toss half around the insides of the prepared tins, coating them lightly. Reserve the remainder.

Add the butter to the processor and whizz for 10 seconds, or until combined with the walnut mixture. Divide the crust among the prepared tins and press firmly over the bases. Put on a baking tray and bake for 10 minutes. Set aside to cool.

Meanwhile, to make the filling, add the ricotta and sugar to the cleaned processor and whizz for 15 seconds, or until smooth. Add the crème fraîche or sour cream, eggs, flour, vanilla and lemon juice and whizz until just combined. Divide the filling among the tins, levelling the surface. Put the tins on the baking tray and bake for 15–18 minutes, or until set.

Cool the tarts in the tins before turning out. Cover the top of each tart with two strips of paper and, using the reserved walnut mixture, dust two parallel lines over the surface.

tip The tarts are delicious served with whipped cream or chocolate ice cream.

index

Published by Murdoch Books Pty Limited

Murdoch Books Australia
Pier 8/9, 23 Hickson Road, Millers Point NSW 2000
Phone: +61 (0)2 8220 2000 Fax: +61 (0)2 8220 2558

Murdoch Books UK Limited
Erico House, 6th Floor North, 93–99 Upper Richmond Road
Putney, London SW15 2TG
Phone: + 44 (0)20 8785 5995 Fax: + 44 (0)20 8785 5985

Chief Executive: Juliet Rogers
Publisher: Kay Scarlett

Concept and art direction: Vivien Valk
Editorial manager: Diana Hill
Project manager: Janine Flew
Editor: Justine Harding
Food editor: Jo Glynn
Designer: Jacqueline Richards
Photographer: Jared Fowler
Stylist: Cherise Koch
Food preparation: Alan Wilson
Recipes by: Sarah DeNardi, Michelle Earl, Jo Glynn, Katy Holder, Louise Pickford,
Wendy Quisumbing, Julie Ray, Diane Temple and the Murdoch Books Test Kitchen
Production: Monika Paratore

National Library of Australia Cataloguing-in-Publication Data: Whizz it. Includes index.
ISBN 1 74045 468 5. 1. Food processor cookery. 2. Cookery. 641.589

Printed by Sing Cheong Printing Co. Ltd. in 2005. PRINTED IN HONG KONG.

IMPORTANT: Those who might be at risk from the effects of salmonella poisoning (the elderly,
pregnant women, young children and those suffering from immune deficiency diseases) should
consult their doctor with any concerns about eating raw eggs.

The Publisher and stylist would like to thank Breville Pty Ltd for lending equipment for use and
photography. They can be found at Breville.com.au

400